FINALLY

Free

FINALLY
Free

Rising Above
Emotional Entrapment

VALENTINA DIMITRI

O'LEARY
PUBLISHING
The Influencer's Press

BONITA SPRINGS, FL

Published in the United States by
O'Leary Publishing
www.olearypublishing.com

ISBN: 978-1-952491-02-3 (print)
ISBN: 978-1-952491-03-0 (ebook)
Library of Congress Control Number: 2020908598

Photography by Louis Venne Photography
Editing by Heather Davis Desrocher and Sharman Monroe
Cover design by Christine Dupre
Book design by Jessica Angerstein

To my beautiful daughter, *Angelika,* my little girl with butterflies in her eyes. Our journey through life has been more than insightful. Through love, tears and laughter we've *grown each other up*. My dearest one, you are loved, more than you know.

To everything there is a season,
a time for every purpose under heaven.

— ECCLESIASTES 3:1-8

CONTENTS

ACKNOWLEDGMENTS

For the creation of this book, my deepest gratitude goes to April O'Leary of O'Leary Publishing, who continually encouraged and inspired me with self-belief and excitement. She kept me elated and energized with the vision of the positive impact this book will have on its readers. But most of all, she made this entire process so much fun! Thank you, April, for believing in me.

To Heather Davis Desrocher, I will be forever grateful for your editing expertise and invaluable input. Your guidance and encouragement, and especially your relentless patience with my not so techie talents, really made this journey possible. Even in my reluctance to make a change, your creative and diplomatic approach always helped me see the light. I learned so much from you. Thank you, Heather. It has been a pleasure working with you.

I especially want to acknowledge and thank my dear brother, Vladimir, for coaching me through the technical snags and glitches anytime of the day or night. Thank you for always responding to my cries of desperation. Without your help, I would still be sitting at this computer. With all my heart, I love having a brother like you.

To my four amazing grandchildren, Stefano, Seraphina, Mia and Gemma, you've inspired me the most. Your excitement and enthusiasm about my writing this book has made this such a fun journey and has kept me dedicated to always being a positive role model for you. "What's the book about, Boonya?" "When will it be finished?" and "I can't wait to read it," are the questions you ask every time you see me. You are like the stars in the sky, twinkling all around me, filling my heart with joy.

To my dearest and most precious friends who've continually supported and encouraged me in the writing of this book, I am forever grateful. Your belief in me has lifted me up to new levels of belief in myself. Thank you, for always being there when I needed lifting. I wish I could name you all. Please forgive me if I missed you. You're still in my heart. Alexandra Jett, Boris Boland, Andrea and Fouad Awada, Jerry Fylonenko, Jane and Andre Mykytenko, Irene Blinderman, Natasha Cuira, Ivy Beshai, Marcelle Raff, Ursula Rosendahl, Joanne Baccile, Franca Jarosz, Vickie Czarnicki, Louise and Bob Campbell, Lydia Jett,

Nina Jett, Natalya Rivers, Nina Sofia Bevier, Victoria Hiller, Lillian and Ray Kelly, Maria Apel, Barbara Jean Harris, Mary McDonough, Louisa Carter, Mary and Richard Snyder, Ina Kacani, Christine and Peter Fylonenko.

I will not leave out my amazing Ukrainian sisterhood of the UNWLA. Thank you to all of you for your warmth, kindness and support. We have grown so much together through our mutual respect and dedication to our cause.

A special acknowledgement for my son-in-law, John, whose friendship and support has always brought peace to my heart. Thank you, John, for all that you do.

PREFACE

Is This Book for You?

Have you asked yourself: *Is this all there is? Am I really happy with my life? Why does this keep happening to me?* Maybe I should be doing something more fulfilling? Do you think that you are doing all the right things, but are just not sure of yourself sometimes? Do you get frustrated, feeling that life is overwhelming? If you have felt this way, or have asked yourself these questions, then this book is for you.

Yes, life can be complicated and stressful, but it doesn't have to be. Could you be stuck in belief patterns that keep you trapped in self-defeating behavior? This book will lead you on a path of self-discovery and transformation so you can *finally free* yourself from *emotional entrapment* and move into the freedom of clarity.

I invite you to join me on a quest to unravel the intricacies of the mind, discover what creates your thoughts, and understand where your beliefs come from. We will explore why we encounter so many obstacles and why we react the way we do. You will be able to answer the questions: *What am I really afraid of and why do I keep finding myself in the same unhappy place?*

What I wish for you, my readers, is to have AHA moments throughout the reading of this book that will answer: *How can I create a more fulfilling life?* You will learn to recognize, and then release, that which has not been serving you and how to connect with the universal creative energy that will bring you the life that you desire.

The subject of this book, Personal Transformation, has been addressed by many fine authors. Each author brings their own perspective on the subject, reaching readers who are energetically aligned with their point of view. Just as there are thousands of musical compositions all using the same twelve musical notes, there are many approaches to the topic of Personal Transformation. I love the process of absorbing many different perspectives on a subject. It gives me a deeper insight and the ability to choose what I feel is right for me.

In this book you will find a step by step approach to understanding human behavior. The many stories that I share give real life examples of overcoming and moving beyond emotional entrapment. Through my own childhood trauma, emotional struggle and personal tragedy, I discovered that there was in me an endless summer in the form of God's guiding light. I experienced this as a sense of protection regardless of what I was facing at the time. There seemed to be a silent communication between this protective energy and me. It made me feel safe, even when I was terribly scared. This communication eventually helped me to recognize the vulnerability in all of us and it ignited my compassion and need to reach out to others.

How Is This Book Different?

It is different in its simplicity, in the clarity of the sentences, and in the organizational format. I write in the way I personally learn best. I write to the novice in all of us, struggling to understand why life is so complicated and wanting to learn how we can make it simpler.

As a teacher, writer and seminar leader, I work from my heart. My objective is not so much to instruct, but to guide my students and readers to have their own experiences of self-discovery. By recognizing your own God-given strengths and abilities, and the belief patterns that may be blocking your growth, you will have the choice to live to your full potential.

This book strives to present material and concepts in a simple, step-by-step approach that facilitates *understanding versus confusion.* The information and exercises in this book are purposefully simple and easy to do, but can be powerfully insightful, and can lead to amazing changes in your life.

Each one of you is unique and you come from your own level of awareness based on your personal life experiences. You will each absorb the information in this book at your own pace and within the scope of your current understanding.

It is my sincere hope that awakening to a new way of thinking - and a newly inspired, stronger, more confident version of yourself - will *finally free* you to embrace your worthiness with love, joy and acceptance. As I often say to my students:

Let me believe it for you,

until you can believe it for yourself.

Unconscious Choices

In the depth of winter, I finally learned that there was in me an invincible summer.

—ALBERT CAMUS

Prelude to a Poem by Portia Nelson

All of our experiences begin with a choice. The choices we make, and the paths we take, are often determined by unconscious, habitual, repetitive behavioral patterns that can leave us confused and troubled. Portia Nelson was a popular American singer, songwriter, and poet of the 1950's who wrote about her struggle to make the right choices. In the following poem, Nelson expresses the conversations going on in her head, her self-talk, as she struggles emotionally to overcome self-defeating behaviors. The poem speaks to the challenge and rewards of making different (and better) choices. Read how Portia Nelson describes her journey.

Autobiography in Five Short Chapters
by Portia Nelson

Chapter 1

I walk down the street.

There is a deep hole in the sidewalk.

I fall in. I'm lost. I'm hopeless.

It isn't my fault.

It takes forever to find a way out.

Chapter 2

I walk down the same street.

There is a deep hole in the sidewalk.

I pretend I don't see it.

I fall in again.

I can't believe I'm in the same place.

But it's not my fault.

It still takes a long time to get out.

Chapter 3

I walk down the same street

There is a deep hole in the sidewalk.

I see it is there.

I still fall in…. It's a habit.

My eyes are open.

I know where I am.

It is my fault!

I get out immediately.

Chapter 4

I walk down the same street.

There is a deep hole in the sidewalk.

I walk around it.

Chapter 5

I walk down another street.

In this poem, what was Portia Nelson trying to tell us about her emotional journey through life? Below is a chapter by chapter interpretation of the painful conversation going on in her head, her self-talk, as she struggles to unravel the confusion of her life decisions. Recognizing her repetitive, self-defeating pattern, in an "Aha" moment of clarity, Nelson opens herself up to the truth of her choices. She is *Finally Free* to rise above her emotional entrapment.

The Self-Talk of *Autobiography in Five Short Chapters*

Chapter 1

My life is so screwed up.

It's hopeless. I'm always in the same mess.

Nothing ever works out for me no matter how hard I try. I just can't get a break. I'm such a failure.

Nobody cares.

Sometimes I just don't know how I'm going to make it through the day.

I'm so drained and overwhelmed with the constant struggle. I just can't do this anymore.

Chapter 2

Here I am again. I guess it shouldn't surprise me.

I thought I did the right thing, but nothing ever changes for me. I'm so discouraged.

Why does this always happen to me?

I was stupid to believe it could get any better.

I should have seen this coming.

I am worthless and nothing good will ever come my way.

Chapter 3

I'm so mad! I can't believe I'm here again.

I thought things were getting a little better.

How did I not see this coming again?

I guess I wasn't paying enough attention.

This must be a pattern.

Somehow I must have created this.

I think I see it now. I get it.

It is my fault. I'm out of here!

Chapter 4

Wow, that was close. I almost fell for that again.

I really shouldn't hang out here anymore.

There is too much temptation here.

I know I've got to make some changes. It's up to me.

I don't want to be here anymore.

I'm never coming back.

Chapter 5

My gosh, it feels so different here.

I'm not so heavy-hearted. I can breathe again.

It's a little scary for me, but I think I like it.

I want to keep going in this direction.

Step-by-step, day-by-day, I'll keep moving forward.

I'll ask for help. I know there are others here who will help me.

More and more, I'm beginning to understand.

It's feeling better every day.

I don't know all the answers yet. There is so much to learn.

I'm sure I'll make mistakes along the way, but if I do,
I'll just dust myself off and keep on going.

I know the way now.

I'm not quitting anymore.

I've been forgiving others and even
forgiving myself.

For the first time in my life I really can say:
I LOVE myself.

I'm Happy, really Happy. I know this because I can't
stop smiling.

Does the story in Portia Nelson's poem sound
familiar? Can you identify, to some degree, with
it for some areas of your life? Most of us spend our
lives repeating themes and patterns of behaviors and
making choices that never bring us good results,
then we wonder why we keep ending up in the same
situation over and over again.

Each time a "repeated" behavior creates a negative
result in our life, it reinforces a deep sense of
unworthiness within us and we begin beating ourselves

up. *See,* we say to ourselves, *this always happens to me. I knew I couldn't do it. Why did I even bother trying?* This kind of self-denigration leaves us wounded and open to more of the same in the future.

Where do our behavior patterns come from and how do we change them? This book will answer these important questions.

Winter

THE SOIL OF OUR PRESENT REALITY

*The season of failure is the best time
for sowing the seeds of success.*

—YOGANANDA

In the winter of our discontent, we can be deeply buried in our troubled emotions with no escape in sight. But deep within our soul are planted the seedlings of hope and inspiration, not yet ready to sprout.

CHAPTER 1

Our Comfort Zone

*The comfort zone may be cozy, but it's hindering
a lot of dreams from coming to fruition.*

—JOHN ASSARAF

Did you know that we have approximately 60,000 thoughts per day and that, for many of us, most of them are negative? Did you also know that the thoughts we are having today are repeats of the thoughts we had yesterday, and the day before that, and the day before that and so on? Our lives are built on the thoughts we carry around in our heads. Unfortunately, most are negative thoughts that we are not even aware of because they have become such a part of our daily self-talk. They include our fears, worries, insecurities, anger, shame, guilt, resentments and blame.

You see, early in childhood we establish beliefs about what is available to us in this world. Those beliefs are based on our innocent interpretations of the input we received from our families, friends, teachers and extended community, much of which was not true. How we are treated and how we are responded to by others, builds our personalities, our attitudes and our perception of our personal value. It's the only input we had to work with. This determines what we think we deserve in life. This is how we build our self-image.

Through this process we build around ourselves and within our mind, a boundary of limitation and put ourselves into a box of limiting beliefs. The walls of this box become our *comfort zone* of habitual behaviors, which creates a barrier to anything outside of those beliefs.

This little box becomes more and more comfortable every day, and everything we do within those *walls*, which we created by our thoughts, have now become *habits* and those habits have become our *reality*.

Even though our box has a door, we rarely venture outside that door for very long because we don't know how to act outside of our box, our comfort zone. We don't know what to expect. We don't know who we might encounter and what they might expect of us. This uncertainty creates fear, tension, anxiety and insecurity. After all, someone may expect us to do something we don't believe we are capable of. Then what would we do?

We may not be happy within our walls, we may not feel fulfilled, we may yearn for a better life, but at least we know how to act and what to expect inside our box and so those walls become our *dark comforters*.

We sit inside our box watching through the window as others build their dreams, achieve their goals and live a happy life and we keep repeating to ourselves what has now become our mantra: *That's all great for them out there, but it's just not possible for me because* (and the litany of reasons begins):

I'll never be successful.

I'm not pretty enough.

I'll never be accepted.

I can't compete with them.

I don't have the money.

I can't afford those things.

I don't have the right education.

I've already tried everything.

I'm too old to start that now.

We say to ourselves, *I'm just not deserving or worthy of anything more.*

So, we make up our minds, at a subconscious level, to only *allow* a certain amount of success and happiness into our lives. Physically, this is all happening in the tiny hypothalamus part of our brain whose job it is to protect us from danger. It does not like change! It views our comfort zone like a set point on a thermostat. So, when we try to make a change, it chemically manipulates our thoughts and emotions in our brain with fear to get us right back into our comfort zone. (more on this process later).

Of course, there are times when our desire and motivation to make a change is so strong that we consciously muster up the will-power to take action toward a desired goal. If we've done enough internal work to have changed some self-defeating behaviors, then maybe we can achieve our goal. But if pursuing our goal takes us too far out of our *comfort zone*, then as we get closer and closer to the edge, tension and anxiety begin to build up. We are often not aware of why, but we begin to lose confidence. We become shaky. Old tapes begin to play in our head and doubt sets in.

Why did I ever think I could do this? We get scared and discouraged and begin finding all sorts of justifiable reasons to sabotage our efforts. We can become really good at justifying. It almost becomes an art. In actuality, it becomes a self-defeating behavior. Some of us go down this road often. I know. I have.

In our effort to create a better life and fulfill our dreams, we think and talk a lot about how and when we are going to make the changes. Yet we never seem to get around to making them. *Why*, we ask ourselves, *do I sabotage myself just when I am getting so close?* It may sound contradictory but, our *inability* to change really has very little to do with our *ability*. Most of us are capable and knowledgeable enough to figure out the steps necessary to achieve a goal. It's not our ability. It's our lack of belief in our ability that holds us back. As Henry Ford said:

> *Whether you think you can or*
> *you think you can't, you're right.*

In the words of Dennis Waitley, author of *The Psychology of Winning*: "It's not what we think we are, that holds us back, it's what we think we are not."

Self-Sabotage: The College Credit Story

Years ago, a close friend of mine had just started college. She chose a major that she was very excited about. She was doing quite well in her classes because she was very bright and very well-read. She was able to hold intelligent discussions on many topics, but by the end of her third year she began having misgivings about her major. Even though she was nearly finished, she was no longer sure that it was the right field for her. So, she chose another major and started all over again.

As my friend approached her third year, she began feeling disillusioned about her choice again. She entered into another program and, by the end of her second year, she simply withdrew from college.

Her grades were excellent and she was often praised by her professors. After eight years in college and with all of the college credits she earned, she had not earned a degree.

Imagination is more important than knowledge. For while knowledge defines all we currently know and understand, imagination points to all we might yet discover and create.

—ALBERT EINSTEIN

Because I knew her history and had observed similar patterns in her past, I recognized this as a classic case of "fear of success." To actually earn a college degree was just too far out of her comfort zone. She was in a pattern of success and sabotage, and just couldn't sustain the feeling of success because she didn't feel worthy of it. This was exactly what I experienced for many years. I passed up several opportunities because I didn't feel worthy.

Comfort Zone

I used to have a comfort zone, where I knew I couldn't fail; The same four walls and busy work, were really more like jail.

I longed so much to do the things I'd never done before, but stayed inside my comfort zone and paced the same old floor.

I said it didn't matter that I wasn't doing much, I said I didn't care for things like titles, praise and such.

I claimed to be so busy with things inside the zone, but deep inside I hoped for something special of my own.

I couldn't let my life go by, just watching others win; I held my breath and stepped aside to watch the change begin.

I took a step and with new strength I'd never felt before, I kissed my comfort zone good-bye, and closed and locked the door.

A step or two, a word of praise, can make your dreams come true. Smile and believe, Success is there for you!

—UNKNOWN

Unfortunately, every time we sabotage our efforts, not only do we <u>not</u> achieve our goal, but we reinforce within our mind that same self-defeating belief. *See, I knew I couldn't do it. Why did I even bother trying?* If you've had a similar experience, do you recall how it made you feel? What is it within us that causes us to sabotage our efforts? Sometimes fear keeps us playing it safe, and sometimes it's our sense of unworthiness. How we perceive ourselves and what we expect for ourselves determines all the choices we make.

Dr. Denis Waitley, a motivational psychologist for U.S. Olympic teams, determined that the most readily identifiable quality of a winner is an overall *attitude* of *positive self-expectancy*. Olympic athletes succeed because they practice *winning* in their imagination. As Napoleon Bonaparte believed, "Imagination is your world and what you see is what you get."

What we expect from ourselves stems from the deeply imbedded beliefs in our subconscious mind. They dictate how we perceive ourselves and how we relate to the world around us. To understand the dynamics of this process, let's look at the interaction between our conscious mind and our subconscious mind.

CHAPTER 2

The Formation of our Beliefs

Until you make the unconscious conscious,
it will direct your life and you will call it fate.

—C.G. JUNG

The beliefs we carry about ourselves come from our self-image, which is actually just a figment of our imagination. We can't see it, we can't hear it, we can't touch, but it holds great power over us. Understanding the mechanics of the formation of the self-image can give us the key to control its power. Let's start by looking at how our mind works.

CHAPTER 2

FUNCTIONS OF THE MIND

SUB-CONSCIOUS MIND

Never sleeps

Keeps the senses functioning

Controls autonomic bodily functions

Houses the memory bank

MEMORY BANK

Stores memories

Records emotions

Gathers information

Can be reprogrammed

Part of the subconscious mind

CONSCIOUS MIND

Evaluates

Makes decisions

Commands the body

Stops functioning during sleep

Uses information from the memory bank

The Subconscious Mind

The subconscious mind has two primary functions. Most importantly, it is responsible for all of our autonomic bodily functions that keep us alive, like our heartbeat, our breathing, our blood flow, etc. It keeps all our senses functioning even when the *conscious* mind is asleep because the *subconscious* mind *never sleeps.* This is very good.

The second function of the subconscious mind is to house the Memory Bank, which stores all of the information ever received *through all our senses* from the moment of birth, and even from time in the womb. Every thought we've ever had, good or bad, everything we've ever heard, true or false, and everything we have seen with our eyes is stored in the memory bank of our subconscious mind. In addition, everything we've imagined, every scent or aroma that we have ever smelled, and everything we physically touched is also stored there. Most importantly, the memory bank also stores every *emotion* that we have associated with each one of those memories. It is these emotions that are triggered when a memory comes up.

This Memory Bank is just like the data in your computer. It simply "stores" the information. Now this is very important. It *does not evaluate* this stored information. Everything there has the same value and significance. Everything you've heard, seen, thought, and imagined is stored as *truth*. In fact, the subconscious mind cannot tell the difference between a real experience and an imagined one. It is said that the subconscious mind can't take a joke because everything it absorbs it takes in as true. We will explore later why this is so significant. But first, let's take a look at the conscious mind.

The Conscious Mind

The conscious mind only functions while you are awake. Its primary function is to make decisions by:

- Gathering information from the memory bank

- Evaluating the information

- Making a judgment

- Commanding the body to take an action

None of the data stored in the memory bank has any power by itself until it is time for the conscious mind to make a decision. The conscious mind must then access the stored information/data from the Memory Bank and make a decision based on what it finds.

Our Programing Controls Our Reality

Let's take a better look at that memory bank, and how it impacts the conscious mind. To do this, let us look at the experience a student has when taking a test. Imagine you are a high school student preparing for a math exam. You say to yourself, *You know, I've never been very good at math. It's been my worst subject and I always do poorly on math exams, but this time it's going to be different because I've been studying with a tutor who's really helped me understand this stuff. I even passed all the self-exams, so I think I'm going to do okay.*

Here's what happens. As soon as the teacher places the test booklet onto your desk, and you see the words, *Math Exam* you look at it and freeze. Suddenly, you can't remember a thing you just learned. Your mind goes blank. Can you guess why this happened? When it was time for the conscious mind to take the test, the information in the memory bank was so overloaded with years of messages like, *"I'm lousy at math," "I hate math," "I always fail math tests,"* etc. These strong messages far outweighed the most recent successes. So, when the conscious mind saw the words *Math Exam* it immediately went into blank mode. This is an example of how our programing controls our reality. This can be overcome, however, as we'll learn later.

Asara Lovejoy, author of *The One Command*, explains it like this:

Everything we perceive is from our own filters of reality *based on and starting with what we perceived from our childhood programming that our subconscious mind took in as truth. We built our belief system based on other people's perceptions, which may or may not have been true. Nevertheless, what was so deeply imprinted on our child's mind are the beliefs we now operate from on auto-pilot.*

Childhood: The Source of Our Beliefs

Our strongest beliefs were formed between the ages of two and seven years old when our minds were mostly in the THETA brain wave state. That's like being in downloaded hypnosis, gathering data from the environment with which to build our belief system. It is when adults and siblings play a crucial role in molding our beliefs about ourselves and our expectations of how life treats us. This is a time when we are very open to suggestions and we believe everything we see and hear. For this reason, it is not a good time to play jokes on children. Since they see everything as true, it confuses them and can frighten them.

This is also the time when we create meaning about ourselves based the behavior of those around us, good or bad. THETA brain waves induce imagination, daydreaming and super-learning. It's when our mind can absorb the most information, which is why young children can easily learn several languages, given the right environment.

> *You can never out-perform your own self-image.*
>
> —MAXWELL MALTZ

As we grow, our brains slowly shift out of theta and move into alpha and beta brainwave frequencies where we become more analytical, we view the world from a broader perspective and adopt critical thinking. However, what was deeply imprinted on our mind while we were in theta continues to exert great power over us.

We Respond To What Our Mind Absorbs

In the early 1900s, the great educator, scientist and first female doctor allowed to practice in Italy, Maria Montessori, studied small children in orphanages. She later wrote a book entitled, *The Absorbent Mind*, where she likened the young child's mind to a sponge that could quickly absorb everything from its environment. At that time, she knew nothing about neuroscience or brain wave states. But even then, over a hundred years ago, she recognized the child's learning process.

Our response to life situations reflects the beliefs our mind absorbed when we were very young. Every feeling or judgement we make is always really *about us and not about them because everything is filtered by what we believe about ourselves.* We create experiences by whom we invite into our lives and we teach people how to treat us by what we allow or think we deserve. We also avoid people and experiences we don't feel worthy of, even though we have a desire to be there.

You see, consciously, we know what we want, but our subconscious programming will often block that desire with thoughts like, *Oh no, that's not for you. You're not smart enough to accomplish that.* Sometimes we get blocked, not by words in our head, but simply by a sense of resistance or discomfort that keeps us from moving forward.

A friend of mine shared an experience and a revelation she once had that speaks to this. She and her friends often frequented a restaurant that they all enjoyed, but every time it was her turn to drive, she noticed that she would get very uncomfortable, anxious, and flushed as they drove up to the valet parking.

After some contemplation on this, she recognized that she simply did not feel worthy of valet parking. It was not what she was used to. In her upbringing that was only for the very elite and wealthy. Even though she was financially very comfortable, she said it made her feel like a fraud and she was afraid to look at the parking attendants because she believed they would recognize that she didn't belong there. This is how powerful our subconscious beliefs can be.

So, if I asked you, "What do you really *want* for yourself?" you would think about it for a while and then give me an answer. But then, if I asked you, "What do you really *expect* for yourself?" would your answer be the same? Think about it. If your answer really is the same, that's wonderful, but most of the time it isn't.

We Get What We Subconsciously Expect,
Not What We Consciously Want.

Until our subconscious *Expectations* can match what we consciously *Want,* the subconscious mind will win every time. What do you expect from your life?

As a quick exercise, make a list with these three columns: *Things I want to do, Things I want to have, Things I want to accomplish.* Fill in items under each heading. After you've finished the list, read over it and put a check mark next to the items you really don't expect to accomplish. Reading through this list will give you some sense of what you really believe is available for you in this life. After each of those check marks, write the words, WHY NOT? We will pursue this idea later in this book.

As we grow and go about our daily lives we slowly *weave* stories within our minds that we act out to others based on the continuous re-surfacing beliefs stored in our memory bank. We weave a story about "who we are" and "what we deserve" in relation to the world around us.

We have a story about different areas of our life. In some areas we see ourselves as successful, happy, confident people feeling really good about ourselves. But in other areas our story could be filled with sadness, discouragement, disappointments, fear and a sense of failure. To recognize if you have a story going on in your life, do some introspection. Consider the next three questions:

In what situations do I find myself in conflict?
In what settings do I often feel like a failure?
Who brings out my anger or insecurity?

In reading these questions, are there answers that come up immediately that give you an emotional charge? If so, those are the areas that really push your buttons. You may want to evaluate them more closely. Look for any deeply imbedded personal beliefs that consistently impact your decisions and actions in a negative way.

On the other hand, you're sure to find stories that bring positive outcomes to your life. That's wonderful and you don't need to be concerned about them, but you do want to be aware of them. It's important to recognize your positive patterns for they can encourage you to continue on that path.

Whatever you
Vividly imagine,
Ardently desire,
Sincerely believe,
And enthusiastically
Act upon.......
Must inevitably
Come to pass!

—UNKNOWN

Now, take a look at the times when you are most discouraged or disappointed in yourself. It's when you catch yourself saying, *Why does this always happen to me?* that can be a signal that there is a strong belief pattern in control there. Ask yourself, *What kind of thoughts and feelings do I carry around in my head most of the time?*

"We live in the feelings of our thinking," says psychologist, Michael Neill, and our stories are what we think about most.

CHAPTER 3

The Stories that Hold Us Hostage

You may not control all the events that happen to you,
but you can decide not to be reduced by them.

—MAYA ANGELOU

Most of us believe that our decisions and actions are based on common sense, everyday reality, in response to circumstances and people in our environment. We don't recognize, however, that it is our emotional response, based on our unconscious beliefs, that really controls our behavior.

We all have childhood stories that formed our beliefs, some of them good and others problematic, and some we are not entirely conscious of. Some of them suck us in more than others. It took me years to finally discover just how much my money beliefs controlled and directed so many of my life decisions. Perhaps the stories that I share with you will help you recognize how your own childhood experiences have impacted your life.

I have two very contradictory stories and each one had great power over me and influenced my money behavior and major decisions in my life.

Messages About Money

In my earliest memory about the purpose of money, I was about seven years old. Sometimes when my father would come home from work, he would play a game with us. He would put his hands in his pockets and pull out the insides so all his change would scatter all over the floor. Then he would say, "Okay, now pick up as much as you can and put it in this box." My younger brother and I had so much fun gathering up all the coins and looking for all the pennies that had rolled down the hall. We were so excited because we knew what was coming.

Next my father would say, "Now take this box of money and run down to the corner store and buy yourself some candy." We were in heaven! So, what I learned from that experience was that money was for having fun and buying stuff that made you happy at the moment.

My second childhood memory of money came several years later when I was about twelve years old. I began to sense that there was something else going on around money. My parents seemed to be concerned about something. I could tell by the stress on their faces, and I could hear them, always whispering about it. I remember it giving me an uncomfortable, unsettling feeling, like something might go wrong at any time. It actually created some fear in me.

One day, as my father was going into the bedroom to pay bills, I remember asking him, "Daddy, how are you going to pay bills in the bedroom?" I was confused because all I knew about paying anything is when you give someone money. I didn't know about writing checks. He turned around abruptly, glared at me and said, "money is none of your business!" I was so stunned because my father never looked at or talked to me that way. I still remember his eyes glaring at me. He was always warm and friendly to me. I had no idea why he responded to me that way, but I never forgot it. I felt like I must have done something terribly wrong.

This incident solidified in me that money was scary! Even though this message was clearly inaccurate and had no validity since I was only twelve years old at the time, it had a *profound impact* on me. I totally believed that handling money was taboo for me and that became the *False Filter*, which I operated from for a very long time.

When it came to finances, I always deferred to others. I avoided handling money like the plague. I proceeded to demonstrate and validate the belief that money was scary throughout my career life, never realizing just how these two incidences contributed to my thinking and decision-making.

Do you recall incidents from your childhood that created false beliefs that have been directing your life decisions? How has this impacted your life?

Altered by Tragedy

Fortunately, I had other stories in my head. I knew I was a good student and I was a hard worker. I had no doubt that I would graduate from college and become a great teacher because that is all I ever wanted to be. But during my senior year of high school, both my parents were diagnosed with cancer. I decided to forgo college for a while and take a job instead.

During the next year, I spent my time working full-time, taking care of my younger brother and visiting each of my parents in and out of hospitals. We had no relatives in the United States so it was all on my shoulders. By the time I was nineteen, both my parents had passed away. My brother was only twelve years old and I knew I had to be strong for him. I put up a pretty good front, trying to keep it together emotionally.

My parents were not wealthy, but they were wise enough to leave us a mortgage-free home, a late model car and some money in the bank.

I now found myself trying to adjust to a new life, without my parents, trying to be responsible and make everyday decisions on my own, decisions I'd never had to make before. I didn't really feel any financial pressures. With my full-time job, and the money my parents had left us we were quite secure.

Actually, I really had no idea what to do with the money I was earning. I was very naïve and completely inexperienced. Unfortunately, my parents never discussed money with me. It was always a hush, hush subject, which is why I always felt so uncomfortable with it. I do remember, shortly after they died, the first electric bill came in the mail. I knew what it was, but I had no idea what to do with it. I actually did not know how to pay a bill. I had to ask a neighbor.

Since I had no real sense of the value of money, I never thought much about saving for the future or saving for emergencies. I had no concept of what that meant. I always had more than I needed. I lived

Stop being afraid of what could go wrong and start being positive about what could go right.

—UNKNOWN

day-to-day and always made sure I had lots of cash on hand. My memory of having so much fun buying all the candy I wanted was all I knew about how and why to spend money.

I became an impulsive buyer and didn't keep very good track of what I was spending. After all, there always seemed to be enough. Remembering that "money was none of my business," I took that to mean that being serious about money and finances was not in my realm of capabilities, but having fun spending it was just fine. I had no clue what being responsible about money really meant.

We live in the feelings of our thinking.

—MICHAEL NEILL

It wasn't too long before my well-meaning friends, in their effort to rescue me, introduced me to a suitable gentleman. He was eight years older than I was, sophisticated, well-educated, with a strong commanding character. He also had no assets, no money, no house and no car, that is, until he married me. As you can imagine, that was the end of my freedom and independence. He became the authority figure and I gladly allowed him to take care of all of my assets. He was now head of household.

Apparently this was more of a comfort zone for me. I wasn't independent long enough to really get into the groove of being independent. In hindsight, I should have given myself more time to grow up. I did end up completing my teaching degree and I earned a Montessori education certification, and I became the mother of a sweet baby girl.

Moving Forward or Not?

With my new credentials, my husband and I decided to start up a private Montessori school, which I was passionate about. He was very helpful and supportive in the setup. That summer, while my in-laws took care of my little girl, I ordered materials, set up the classrooms, created lesson plans, set up an office and studied state regulations for state licensure. I created marketing materials and went out into the community to recruit students. These were all things I had never done before.

After seven years, we had three very successful and profitable private schools. I was teaching and running the schools and he and our accountant were handling the finances. Our marriage, however, was not very successful.

During the divorce proceedings, he convinced me that I would never be able to handle the finances of even one school. He always intimidated me, and I wasn't strong enough to stand up to him. As much as I loved the schools and all the success I experienced, my self-belief was just not strong enough. The fear of handling finances freaked me out and I walked away from all three successful schools with nothing to show for seven years of hard work.

What I did know about myself, however, was that I was resourceful, capable, a quick learner, and I soon found myself in a whole new career. I was still in the education arena, but now at the high school level, creating career centers. Later, I moved to the college level and then to a university where I became the director of the Graduate Career and Placement Department. It was at this time that I met a delightful, warm, friendly and very handsome professional man. He was enamored by me, supportive of my interests and respected my professional accomplishments. It was easy to trust him, and we were soon married.

> *If you're always trying to be normal, you'll never know how amazing you can be.*
>
> —MAYA ANGELOU

We got along very nicely for several years and, of course, as was my pattern, I was very happy to relinquish all our financial affairs to him (after all, money was none of my business) and he was very willing to accommodate. In fact, he accommodated so well that he gambled away everything we owned. *I was devastated!* I had no idea he was a closet gambler. He hid it so well. After seventeen years of marriage, I lost my house and all my savings. I was now in debt, and when I left, I only had my car and my job. I moved in with a girlfriend to get my life back together. Luckily, my daughter was now in college. I was not yet recognizing the belief pattern I was living in.

I was still walking down the same street and falling into that same hole.

Enlightenment Begins

I must have been a very slow learner, but my eyes were open now! I made a commitment to change my life. I started to really pay attention. I began recognizing the patterns of behavior that kept me in a cycle of *success and sabotage* and the emotions like fear, guilt, shame and insecurity that triggered those behaviors. I knew there was something about my thinking, my internal negative self-talk, that triggered emotions that lead to wrong decisions, the *false filters*. I realized that I had bought into a life of struggle because I didn't feel worthy of happiness and well-being. But I soon learned that I could change, that it really was possible for me. I could walk down another street. I was now on a journey into self-discovery and *Transformation*. I began reading voraciously, going to support groups, listening to tapes, taking classes, journaling and attending seminars. At one of my jobs, I was trained to teach motivational classes. I was completely committed to letting go of my fears and insecurities and taking charge of my life. Growth is a never-ending journey, but every step forward is so rewarding and uplifting.

CHAPTER 3

Examining Your Life

What kind of stories have you been living and how have they directed your life?

To embark on your own journey of renewal, self-discovery and transformation, I invite you to begin by writing your own story. Noting the triggers of past recollections and experiences, you can discover the beliefs behind them and how they have impacted your life decisions.

- Start by simply listing recollections of experiences.

- Do not worry about the sequence of events. This can stop the flow of thoughts coming in.

- You do not need to do this in one sitting. Make it an on-going adventure.

- Choose a particular time of the day to spend 20-30 minutes writing and reflecting.

- Always begin by getting comfortable and relaxing with a few slow deep breaths.

- You may find that while recalling events, suddenly you will just want to keep writing. You'll be in the flow of memories and won't be able to stop. This is extremely therapeutic.

As you write your story, note past decisions you made in different circumstances. Can you see patterns of behaviors emerging? Were there times when you really excelled and felt good

> *Life is not determined by what we are given, but by how we choose to use it.*
>
> —ANONYMOUS

about yourself? Now note the times when your decisions and behaviors seemed to always bring you down. It's the *patterns* that are significant here. It's when you can say, "Oh my gosh, I never realized that about myself before," is when you begin asking yourself, "What have I been believing about myself all this time?" The best way to release your old story is to first recognize what it is.

Identifying our stories allows us to evaluate who we've been, who we are and who we really want to be. It gives us a framework and a path to move forward on.

The Power of Beliefs

WANT	EXPECT
Conscious	Unconscious

We Get What We Subconsciously Expect
Not What We Consciously Want.

Until We Can Shift Our
Negative Sub-Conscious
Beliefs, So They Are Intune with
Our Conscious Desires,
This Pattern Will Continue.

Spring

WHAT SEEDS WERE PLANTED?

And the day came when it was more painful to stay tight in the bud, than the risk to blossom.

—ANAIS NINN

While winter thaws, the growing warmth of the spring sun shines life onto the embryo seedlings of hope and inspiration, preparing for growth and transformation.

CHAPTER 4

Fear and Desire

*Too many of us are not living our dreams
because we're too busy living our fears.*

—LES BROWN

Life never stands still. Change is always happening.
We are all seekers; it's in our nature. We all have desires
and DESIRE is the energy that makes the world move.
Desire is what gives our energy direction. If no one ever
wanted anything, there would never be any change at
all. There would be no purpose, and life would cease

to exist. Like a beautiful flower that seeks the sunlight because it desires nourishment, we are nourished by the fulfillment of our desires and dreams. They are what give our life purpose. Desires create ideas and ideas create growth, change and ultimately expansion.

Yet, if change is such a constant, why are we so afraid of it? We all have areas in our life we would like to change yet sometimes the thought of going there immobilizes us. Deep inside us all is the realization that our life could be more fulfilling, but our programmed beliefs keep us stuck in disbelief. Of all the *judgements* we make, the one most critical to our success and happiness is the judgement we make about ourselves.

Dennis Waitley tells us there are really only two motivators in life: Fear and Desire. The judgments we make about ourselves determine the choices we will make. *Fear holds us back*, but *desire moves us forward.* Let me share how clearly, Fear and Desire played out for me.

My Cheesecake Story

The summer I left the Montessori schools, while waiting for my new position in the fall, I was invited to a business luncheon hosted by a friend of mine who was a supervisor of a large department store chain. This was an annual event she hosted for the managers of all the stores in the area. She asked if I would be willing to bake a few of my special cheesecakes for the ladies to sample. She loved my cheesecakes and I loved baking. So, of course I agreed.

They were such a success that I received several requests to bake cheesecakes for a variety of events. Then someone suggested that I start a small home-based business, something that I had never thought to do. The idea sounded so appealing and I was getting such great feedback, which boosted my confidence. I had the time to do it, so I decided to go for it. I had already started one successful business so I was pretty sure I could do it again. I was very enthusiastic, and I started dreaming about how successful it could be.

Now I was on fire, and I wasn't going waste any time. So, I rolled up my sleeves and went right to work. I sat down and began making a list of all the materials and equipment I would need. I looked up wholesalers I would buy from and began purchasing more baking pans and special boxes for delivery. I made lists of people and organizations I would sell to and began thinking about building a new kitchen in my basement, all the while getting more orders through word of mouth for cheesecakes.

I was so happy, and by now convinced, that I was doing the right thing. I needed a name and logo for my new business, so I sat down with pen and paper and began drawing a little mouse and next to the mouse was a big slice of cheesecake with a bite taken out of it. He was such a cute little mouse. As I sat admiring my new logo, the name: The Cheesecake Factory came to me (sound familiar?). I loved the name and decided to keep it. I was going to order stickers with my new name and logo on it to put on the boxes I had ordered.

In my enthusiasm, I began telling my friends and others about my new business venture. I don't even remember who it was I only remember the words, "Are you crazy? You can't do this. It will never work for

Never let anybody tell you where you can't go, especially if they haven't been there yet.

—LES BROWN

you. You're going to need a commercial oven. Then you'll have to have state inspections. Do you know much this is going to cost you?"

In all of my enthusiasm and the positive feedback I had been getting, it just took one negative encounter to stop me in my tracks! Desire had been moving me forward in a wonderful new direction, but the fear of failure, fear of being judged and looking foolish, halted all my effort. My fragile self-image and the pattern of not believing in myself was still there, still controlling my decisions. In my wavering faith, I stopped making cheesecakes and abandoned the business.

About six months later, I was driving through another part of town some distance away when I noticed a small storefront with the words, The Cheesecake Factory. Sadly, I thought of my lost dream and wondered if, somehow, the name that I wasn't ready to claim showed up for someone else who was ready. Later I discovered that the storefront I passed was the original Cheesecake Factory that has now grown nationally into a multi-million-dollar business.

The moral of this story is: *Never let anyone take away your dream.*

Do you have your own version of The Cheesecake Story?

Fear and Desire

Fear holds us back. Desire moves us forward.

When we make a decision from *fear* we feel a risk

of some sort, anxiety, discouragement and a loss of self-esteem. It's a lower, heavier feeling.

When we make a decision from *desire* we feel hopeful, and enthusiastic as we envision a positive desired outcome. This is a lighter, uplifting feeling.

Desire is usually easy to recognize, but Fear often comes in disguise and overcomes us before we can recognize it. Fear is an invisible, negative, repelling force whose main objective is to *stop* us from fulfilling our desires. Fear shows up in behaviors such as: procrastination, indecisiveness, resistance, hesitation, justification, avoidance, making excuses, rationalizing and self-doubt.

Becoming aware of these behaviors and recognizing them as "fear in disguise" allows us to catch ourselves and begin identifying what kind of fear we are feeling. This is very helpful in identifying our own self-defeating behaviors.

Do you have a fear of rejection, fear of failure, fear of judgement? *Guilt* and *shame* are often associated with these fears. Are these emotions sabotaging your success? What kind of fears do you feel?

> *Let your choices reflect your hopes, not your fears.*
>
> —NELSON MANDELA

Although we are not usually consciously aware of it, in almost all of our behaviors and interactions is an underlying need, something that seems to pull us into a behavior, that *validates*, *substantiates*, and *perpetuates* our subconscious beliefs about ourselves. This can be helpful or harmful to us depending on the subconscious beliefs we have formed.

If we grew up in a highly supportive environment with lots of positive feedback then we will probably, for the most part, display self-confidence and positive behaviors that create successful outcomes. But if like many of us, we grew up with self-defeating messages along the way, our behaviors, attitudes and interactions will reflect how we interpreted those messages.

So, whatever we believe about ourselves at a subconscious level, we will continue to recreate by our actions and attitudes. If you believe you are not worthy, you will demonstrate a behavior that validates your unworthiness to others and give them permission to treat you accordingly. Then you think, "See, I knew I was no good; nobody really likes me." This justifies your belief. In doing so, you perpetuate the cycle. The power of our personal belief system is immense.

Below are a few classic examples of self-defeating behaviors and the *subconscious* beliefs that they may stem from:

Perfectionism – We will never be perfect, yet we keep striving to make everything perfect. This perpetuates the belief that we will never be good enough to compete with others and live the life that we desire.

Always observing, never participating – feeling like an outsider, fear of failure, never feeling good enough or feeling we do not belong, not wanting to be noticed, feeling embarrassed.

Being a spend-thrift, always blowing money – perpetuating a belief of always being broke, not feeling worthy of being wealthy, thereby spending money impulsively on things that have no value, having a "poor me" mentality.

All or nothing behavior - avoiding paying a debt until you can pay it all back; avoiding starting a project until you can complete it all at once; perpetuating the belief that you are irresponsible, can't be counted on, don't follow through, are not trustworthy, needing to prove you are a loser.

Always making excuses - not taking responsibility for being late, finding rationale for not completing an assignment, believing you're a victim of circumstances, that things never go your way, that you're irresponsible.

Allowing yourself to be pulled into distraction - taking on more than you can handle, making unimportant things important, not able to say no, believing you never have enough time, needing to feel important or valued because you are always busy, needing approval of others, needing to justify why you can't get things done.

Attention to detail in excess - constantly re-doing, re-writing, and re-starting, taking far more time than needed on any project, overdoing anything – fear of being judged, fear of not being good enough, excessive need for approval (usually related to tasks or assignments at school or at work).

Avoiding dealing with money - ignoring your bills, not paying attention to your spending, avoiding looking at your bank account, fear of lack, afraid to face reality, living in a fantasy, playing a victim.

Blaming others - fear of being judged, fear of being found out, feeling inadequate, being irresponsible, believing you're a victim.

Procrastination - putting off tasks, not believing in your own worthiness to do the right thing, fear of failure, needing to prove that you're incapable.

We are what we repeatedly do. Excellence then, is not an act, but a habit.

—ARISTOTLE

We've all behaved in the ways listed in most of these above categories, but it's the excessive patterns we need to recognize and address. As you read through the above ten behaviors, which ones ignited emotions within you? Did you have to question yourself and ask, "Do I really do this?" Go through them once again, this time more slowly. Can you identify any repetitive behaviors? If so, you may want to examine how they are affecting your life. Do you see any patterns here?

Pattern of Being

SUBCONSCIOUS PROGRAMMING

Creates Our

BELIEFS

Which Trigger Our

THOUGHTS

Which Ignite Our

EMOTIONS

Which Are Demonstrated By Our

BEHAVIOR

Which Create Our

REALITY

We all live within a pattern of behavior. The pattern is always the same, but the behavior varies from person to person. All of our behaviors impact the quality of our life.

CHAPTER 5

Living in the Feelings of Our Thinking

*Whatever you believe about yourself on the inside
is what will manifest on the outside.*

—UNKNOWN

As we have learned, our beliefs were formed early on during the programming of our subconscious mind. Does this mean that we are permanently imprinted and limited by the boundaries of that programming? Fortunately, there is another dynamic that comes into play here:

CHAPTER 5

Energy

You see we are all energetic beings living in an electro-magnetic field. Everything we think, feel, say and do sends out a vibration that either feels good, feels bad or is somewhere in between. The vibrations of our thoughts and feelings create the reality that we live in. Let us explore how this works.

According to modern day physicists, our whole world is an electro-magnetic field of energy where

Like Attracts Like
Thoughts ignite emotions, which then attract experiences or situations of the same magnetic frequency.

physical matter and energy are one. Thoughts carry an electrical charge and emotions are magnetic waves. The nature of energy is motion so everything in the universe is made up of vibrating waves with individualized frequencies. It's an *attracting* energy because it's magnetic. Our bodies also vibrate magnetically, as do the emotions that carry the waves.

So, if we maintain a positive attitude most of the time, we create positive outcomes. On the other hand, if we carry negative attitudes and stay in a bad mood most of the time, we can't expect a positive outcome. We usually get what we expect, and then we call it bad luck. Moment by moment, we are actually creating our circumstances by the magnetism of what we are *feeling*. Unfortunately, many of us believe that we have no control over our feelings, and, therefore, we relinquish control of our circumstances and live in victimhood. But since our feelings are triggered by our thoughts, we *can* learn to think "better feeling thoughts."

Choose Upliftment

When we think an uplifting thought, it will fill us with a positive emotion. We feel good about ourselves and more confident. In our confidence we are more open to new ideas. New ideas are the beginning of creating something new. We see opportunities and are more willing to look for solutions and take risks rather than focus on failure. We stay open-minded and become excited about new possibilities that, in a bad mood, we may not have entertained. Following up on that opportunity, could lead to a wonderful experience. This State of Mind keeps us in charge of our own well-being and happiness.

Focused on Problems?

On the other hand, when we focus on problems most of the time, our mind stays in the problems. We feel stressed, annoyed, irritated, angry and overwhelmed. This kind of energy shuts us down. It exhausts us. It does not allow us to be creative or use our imagination for our dreams and desires. It's not open to new possibilities. Everything seems to go wrong.

When we feel drained, we can't see solutions. We don't believe they exist for us. We keep rehearsing the same scenario over and over again, like being on a treadmill. Our self-confidence diminishes and this immobilizes us. We become discouraged and often begin comparing ourselves to others, believing that they have a better life than we do. Then we blame them for not understanding us.

What are You Vibrating?

This is how *like attracts like* It all starts with the magnetic energy of an emotion, precipitated by a thought. What do you think about most of the time? What kind of mood are you in most of the time? Seminar leader, Mary Morrissey, often says, "Notice what you're noticing and practice noticing the positive." What we notice is what we put our energy on. We draw to ourselves more of whatever we give attention to on a regular basis. When we are in a negative State of Mind, like radar, we get drawn to anything that will reinforce or justify the negative emotion we are feeling at that moment. This only perpetuates that emotion and extends the feeling until we work ourselves into frenzy. Over a long period of time this scenario can be damaging to our health.

Speaker and best-selling author, Joe Vitale, puts it this way,

It's really important that you feel good. Because this feeling good is what goes out as a signal into the universe and starts to attract more of itself to you. So, the more you can feel good, the more you can attract things to yourself that will help you feel good and that will keep bringing you up higher and higher.

So, when you catch yourself in a bad mood, take a deep breath, readjust your posture and smile. Focus on something that you're grateful for, your child, the sunshine, the flowers in your garden, the freedom to breathe, your warm cozy bed. Gratitude is considered one of the highest energy frequencies and it will always lighten your mood.

Our bodies send out electro-magnetic waves every second of every day and those magnetic waves return to us the circumstances in our life that are a vibrational match to what we just sent out with our emotions. It's usually what we already expect because, most of the time, we're feeling the same emotions over and over again. It's because we are thinking the same thoughts day after day after day (about 60,000 a day). Observe how many of them are positive thoughts and how many are negative thoughts.

Are You Stuck in a Pattern?

Many of us hold on to the same damaging emotions for weeks, months and even years. These thoughts then ignite the same negative vibratory emotions such as anger, frustration, sadness, disappointment, and feelings of unworthiness and on and on.

This never-ending cycle of thought and feeling creates a pattern of behavior. It creates our everyday reality over and over again until something in our life causes us to wake up and make a conscious change.

The chains of habit are too weak to be felt until they are too strong to be broken.

—SAMUEL JOHNSON

This could be a slowly growing discontent that finally brings to recognition that somehow our life just isn't working well. This conscious awareness of our own discontent can give us insights into beliefs we may not be aware that we have. Awareness is the first step to creating something new and something better.

So, at what frequency are you vibrating? If you don't know, simply ask yourself, *What am I usually feeling? Am I generally in a good mood or not?* The vibration of that feeling is attracting to you the life circumstances that you are living. Is it bringing you the life you want? Are you vibrating in joy or in fear?

Since 1915, Albert Einstein's *Theory of Relativity* introduced a whole new way of viewing the world.

The fact that energy and matter are one and the same is precisely what Einstein recognized when he concluded that E=mc2. Simply stated, this equation reveals that energy (E)= mass x speed of light squared (C2). Einstein revealed that we do not live in a universe with discrete, physical objects separated by dead space. The universe is one indivisible, dynamic whole in which energy and matter are so deeply entangled it is impossible to consider them as independent elements.

—BRUCE H. LIPTON, *The Biology of Belief: Unleashing The Power of Consciousness, Matter and Miracles*

To help you shift your experience of a person or a situation that consistently distresses you, use the following exercise.

The Example of My Sister

In the left column, list what really bothers you about the person or situation. Be specific so that your mind is very clear about this problem.

Now take some time to think about how you would really like it to be. List anything that you desire in the situation. Begin your list, but make sure you put everything in the affirmative and in the present. For example: "I love how my sister always cleans up after herself."

When your list is completed, take a look at the left column and draw an X all the way through it. Time to create a new reality. Now fold the paper in half, lengthwise and begin reading the "How you would like it to be" column over and over to yourself, while visualizing it in your mind. Continue reading out loud for at least thirty days and notice how things begin to change. Stay positive and be grateful.

The following is an interesting way to look at the way things are now, as opposed to the way you would like them to be:

The Art of Attraction
by Abraham/Hicks

Practice the Art of Allowing which means reaching for the thought that feels the best, not the thought that is the real thought, not the thought that is telling it like it is now.

Telling it like it is now only holds you where you are now. But everyone expects me to tell it like it is. If you like it as it is, then tell it like it is. But if you don't like it as it is, then tell it like you want it to be.

If you tell it like you want it to be long enough, you will begin to feel it like you want it to be. And when you feel it like you want it to be long enough, It will become like you want it to be.

Please use the self-assessment section at end of book to help you determine your self-defeating beliefs so you can overcome them.

We are not victims of our genes, but masters of our fates, able to create lives overflowing with peace, happiness and love.

—BRUCE H. LIPTON, PHD

CHAPTER 6

The Emotional Elevator

I was exhilarated by the new realization that I could change the character of my life by simply changing my beliefs. I was instantly energized because I realized there was a science-based path that would take me from my job as a perennial "victim" to my new position as "co-creator" of my destiny.

—BRUCE H. LIPTON, PHD

We all experience a range of emotions and sometimes life can feel like we are living on an elevator, which is constantly moving up and down. Where we are on the elevator depends on what we are experiencing at the moment and the thoughts we are having about the experience.

Our emotions can be the very low, heavy feelings like *grief, despair and powerlessness.* These vibrations are very slow moving and make our bodies feel heavy and sluggish. Our bodies demonstrate low, heavy feelings with slouching shoulders, a hanging head, and a frowning face.

Our words demonstrate this when we say things like, "I'm really down today," or "I'm feeling heavy-hearted." On these days it's even hard to fake a smile. As we move up the elevator, our energy begins to slowly lighten. Even emotions like *worry, doubt and disappointment* will feel better than *powerlessness.*

If we continue to move higher and higher, feeling better and better, our whole demeanor will begin to change because now we are vibrating at a much faster and lighter rate and our bodies feel uplifted and we begin to smile. That's because we are feeling emotions like *optimism* and *hope*. We say things like, "I'm so excited." Now, instead of saying, "heavy-hearted," we can say, "I'm feeling light-hearted." We don't always realize it, but our words and our body really do express how we are vibrating at any given moment.

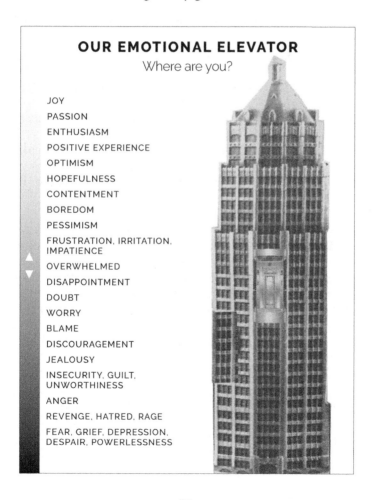

OUR EMOTIONAL ELEVATOR

Where are you?

JOY

PASSION

ENTHUSIASM

POSITIVE EXPERIENCE

OPTIMISM

HOPEFULNESS

CONTENTMENT

BOREDOM

PESSIMISM

FRUSTRATION, IRRITATION, IMPATIENCE

OVERWHELMED

DISAPPOINTMENT

DOUBT

WORRY

BLAME

DISCOURAGEMENT

JEALOUSY

INSECURITY, GUILT, UNWORTHINESS

ANGER

REVENGE, HATRED, RAGE

FEAR, GRIEF, DEPRESSION, DESPAIR, POWERLESSNESS

Notice the wide range of emotions depicted on the diagram of "Our Emotional Elevator" (and there are many more). We've probably all experienced most of these emotions - maybe not the lowest and maybe not the highest, but we know the difference between feeling good, feeling badly and feeling better.

We each have a *signature* vibration, or set of emotions, that fluctuates up and down within a certain range, like a set point. This is our State of Mind. These are the thoughts and feelings we carry around with us, *most of the time*. Even if we don't express them, it shows in our mood.

Our State of Mind influences our attitudes, our moods, our personality and what we really expect to get out of life. It's from the vibration of our set point that we draw, or attract, circumstances to ourselves. It's how we *create our own reality* because what we strongly feel, and consistently think and say, will expand. It's *energy*.

Absorbing Our Environment

When we are very young, we have no filters, no way of logically processing our emotional responses or behaviors to outside stimuli or experiences. We simply feel the energy of whatever is happening around us or the energy of someone interacting with us.

We interpret our whole environment with our senses and the feeling in our body. Every cell in our body feels the vibrations. We know when something feels good or when something feels bad. We absorb through all the senses, like a sponge, and those feelings become deeply imbedded memories.

We feel love and we can sense danger and every feeling in between. The good energy of a hug makes us smile. The energy of a stern word or a shout can startle us and make us cry. This is all stored in our subconscious mind.

As babies or toddlers when we hear words, we interpret the feeling, not the meaning of the words.

CHAPTER 6

We don't really *think* because we need words to have a thought. For instance, you can enjoy a beautiful sunset with all of your senses, but you can't think about the sunset without words. Once we begin using words, it's almost impossible to enjoy the view and to not think, *How beautiful.* So, when mommy enters the baby's room, baby doesn't think, *Oh, mommy is here,* with all its senses. It just knows mommy is here, like radar. As we grow we begin relying much more on our thinking brain.

Building Our Beliefs

When we mature, our childhood programming slowly expands into a broader belief system of how we currently see the world and those around us, in relation to who we have come to believe we are.

All the interactions that we have encountered along the way have added an additional dimension to our belief system. Do we live in a friendly world or a hostile world? Do people accept us or not? What we believe about how people interact with us, shapes how we see ourselves.

Creating Our Identity

By this time, we have become emotionally grounded in our habitual reactive behaviors, and our memorized thoughts and emotions. Our reactions to conflicts usually have more to do with how we perceive ourselves than the situation itself. We have now bought into a belief system of how things are, and how we fit into this world, and who we believe we are in relation to others.

Addicted to What's Wrong

We cling to that belief for dear life. We fiercely defend it, because it has now become our *identity*. We already know how to behave here and how we should show up in the world. Since we don't know any other way, who would we be if we didn't have the story of our identity? How would we know how to act if we tried to change it? The idea of it can create a great deal of fear and anxiety. So, we simply become addicted to our problems. It's all we know, which is why we often recreate them.

When all we focus on is what's wrong, it's the only thing that can keep returning. Have you ever met someone who is always looking to find something wrong, and if they can't find it, they often create it? If you have, you probably know what I mean. Being in a situation that is trying to pull us out of our comfort zone can be very scary. The self-image and beliefs that we absorbed through our programming now dictate our personality and our entire demeanor. "It's who I am," you say even if you don't like yourself.

> *Energy flows where attention goes.*
>
> —UNKNOWN

Through this habitual behavior, we are now living *unconsciously* within the range of emotions that have become our State of Mind. We're having the same thoughts today that we had yesterday and the same emotional reaction to them that we had yesterday. It has now become a cycle and it will continue to "*recreate our past and never bring us a new future.*" As the saying goes, "Same old, same old," or "If nothing changes, nothing changes." This is why we often hear the complaint, "Why does this always happen to me?" This puts us in a place of powerlessness and makes us feel like a victim. Let's examine another really important factor that keeps this cycle going.

Emotions That Control Us

Look again at the diagram on page 91. Can you determine the range of emotions you are feeling most of the time? Keep in mind that there are times when we do move far above our range and also times when we drop down to a much lower point. Draw a circle around the range of emotions you believe you feel or respond from most of the time.

Are there one or two emotions that you're always feeling? Now, take some time to do some introspection. Look at each emotion within that circle and try to remember the last time you felt that feeling. Was this a good feeling or not? What were the circumstances? What specifically triggered the feeling? Who else was involved? How often do you experience this feeling?

Let's use the emotion, irritation, for example. This can give you a gauge to work with. Ask yourself:

How often do I get irritated?

How often do I say to myself or others, "That really irritates me?"

What triggers my irritation?

Is it a particular person or is it a particular situation or am I just always irritated?

Do this with each of the emotions in the circle you drew.

Becoming the Observer

Becoming aware or conscious of how you actually respond to life on a regular basis requires *paying attention on purpose.* Since we spend most of our days performing our tasks on autopilot, we are not always fully aware of the emotions we are actually feeling. Here is an experiment that I often do to monitor my emotions.

When I'm driving by myself I keep the radio off and continue driving in silence. Try this yourself. Try to keep your mind clear and focus only on your driving. You will find that it's next to impossible to keep thoughts from rushing in. So, begin paying attention to the nature of the thoughts coming in. Since you are alone, this is a good time to do this. Ask yourself, *What am I thinking?* How would you label these thoughts - good, bad, happy, sad, and stressful? How are you feeling? Are you peaceful and relaxed, tense and anxious or sad and worried? All these feelings have a frequency. Try to name the emotions you are feeling. What's going on in your body?

When we begin to consciously pay attention to what's going on in our head we actually become more acquainted with ourselves. We begin having AHA moments. We question, we evaluate, we create a clearer picture of who we are and where we want to be and the circumstances we would like to change.

This is an easy exercise to do anytime you are driving alone. Try to do it often because it will show you what kind of mood you are in most of the time. It allows you to determine what is triggering certain behaviors, who is really pushing your buttons, and why you respond the way you do.

See if you can recognize a pattern. Keep a pad of paper in the car so you can record any insights you have. (Only write after you've stopped, of course.)

The Vibration of Our Emotions

Self-awareness is the first step on the road to transformation and it helps us to evaluate and question how we have been living our life. If we don't take the time to examine what we've been thinking, what we've been feeling, and our reactions to them, we will simply find ourselves being victims living on autopilot and responding to our reactive emotional patterns.

The vibrations of our emotions create the circumstances we find ourselves in. Are we happy and content with our circumstances or do we desire to change them? We need to make conscious choices about the actions we take, moving from reaction to conscious action.

CHAPTER 6

Focus on Your Desires

Many of us are looking for a more fulfilling life, whether it's a better relationship, more money, greater health, a nicer job or the ability to develop a desired talent. All of our desires are available to us if we can just tune in to the frequency of the positive energy available to us. You've already learned that as energetic beings we are always vibrating. Therefore, we are always creating based on the frequency and nature of our vibration. Anything that we desire, we need to *feel into being.*

If you truly want to manifest something new in your life, it requires a strong desire to do so and a willingness to stay focused and vigilant about keeping negative thoughts from entering your mind and speaking only in positive terms. Watch your vocabulary! Every word we speak or think has a frequency behind it. Because we are creatures of habit, it is easy to neutralize our positive intentions with negative thoughts that are always trying to creep back in. It's easy for our buttons to get pushed and suddenly, without realizing it, we are in the midst of anger, blame and negativity.

When this happens and you catch yourself, simply stop and say, "Oops, there I go again." Don't go into blame. That just keeps you in a negative cycle. Be kind and re-commit yourself to your goal. Then, as the Rev. Jack Boland, a friend of mine, used to say, "Just keep on keeping on." And, "Never give up," as Napoleon Hill used to say.

You cannot create a new future with the emotions of the past.

—DR. JOE DISPENZA

In every new day is an opportunity for a new and exciting change. Just practice choosing *better feeling thoughts* and connect to the *deep desire* within your heart. We are all a continuous work in progress.

Believe in yourself and know that everything is possible.

Summer

GROWING AND BLOOMING

The Rainbows of Summer, a treasure of light,
a reflection of hope, an uplifting sight.

Under the vast summer sky, new thoughts and fresh ideas are blooming everywhere. Hope fills the air with the inspiration of all the colors of the rainbow, growing us in every direction.

CHAPTER 7

Body, Mind and Emotions

When you change your thoughts, you can change
everything, including your physiology.

—DR. WAYNE DYER

There is another very important reason to make
positive changes in our lives. Recent studies in cellular
biology and neuroscience have discovered that every
thought we have, has a chemical reaction in our
brain, which triggers our hormones to create certain
emotions in our mind and body.

Thoughts Evoke Emotions

We think of emotions as something we only feel in our mind, yet our bodies respond accordingly with knee-jerk reactions, heart palpitations, body tensions, trouble breathing, nausea, relaxation, exhaling in relief, feeling flushed, sudden headaches, sweaty palms, rapid heartbeat, rising blood pressure, and becoming red in the face.

We also say things like, "Just the thought of that makes me shiver," or "I get nauseous when I step into that room," or "Holding his hand makes me tingle all over," or "My heart was pounding so hard when it was my turn to say my lines." We have all experienced these kinds of bodily reactions. And these are just the reactions we are aware of. There are other responses within our bodies that we are not even aware of.

Addicted to Feeling Badly?

As we've already learned, thoughts are very powerful. They can actually evoke the same emotions and physical manifestations as a real experience. That is why it is very important to be vigilant and stay aware of the thoughts we allow to live in our mind over long periods of time because it will affect our bodies.

Our body actually holds on to these emotions. If we keep a positive outlook on our life circumstances, it will help to keep us healthier. On the other hand, if we spend years repeatedly holding onto negative thoughts and feelings, and the emotions evoked by those thoughts, we will continue to create the same chemical reaction in our brain.

Over the years, shifting into emotional reactions becomes easier and easier because we have formed deep neural pathways in our brain just for them. Our body has actually memorized those emotions and the behaviors they evoke. These habitual negative thoughts and emotions can actually become addictive because of the stimulating sensation of the chemical release that comes with it, just like any drug.

We often, on a subconscious level, recreate dramas and scenarios in order to feel certain feelings despite the fact that they don't feel good. We can actually be addicted to feeling bad because we crave the chemical release that has become part of our negative reactions.

Your thoughts are the architects of your destiny.

—DAVID O. MCKAY

According to Dr. Joe Dispenza, author of *Breaking the Habit of Being Yourself*, when someone pushes your button, it's because you've spent most of your life responding to a *memorized set of behaviors* triggered by the repetition of the same thoughts, beliefs, perceptions and attitudes which come from our subconscious programming. Once our responses become habitual, they become automatic patterns of behavior that we are not always consciously aware of. Dr. Dispenza describes this as "the body becoming the mind." As the body begins to crave the stimulating sensation of the chemicals released by certain emotions, it's the body that begins to direct our behavior, not the mind.

Not So Sweet

A personal example of this is how I used to respond to stressful encounters. When my button was pushed and the tension in my body began to build up, I was suddenly overwhelmed with a strong craving for something sweet. Sometimes it was so overpowering that I would go into a frenzy searching for something sweet to eat. If I couldn't find anything, I would jump into my car and drive to the store, usually to get some ice cream.

During this time, I was still feeling tension and anxiety, especially in my throat. The tension would not subside until I had eaten the whole carton, and could finally take a deep breath. Afterwards, I couldn't believe what I had just done, and I would ask myself, *Why did I do that?* I couldn't really understand what compelled me to react that way, and I would get so angry at myself. I felt so defeated, discouraged and powerless. Knowing that I didn't seem to have any control over that behavior, I would move into depression and erode my self-esteem a little bit more. Does this scenario sound familiar to some of you?

It's not your aptitude, but your attitude that determines your altitude.

—ZIG ZIGLAR

This is a perfect example of how the body becomes the mind. The cravings of my body ignited the behavior. I didn't consciously say to myself, "I'm so upset about this, I should go get some ice cream." No, my behavior was led by a strong conditioned impulse. It is what Dr. Joe Dispenza calls "a memorized behavioral response to a certain stimulus." This is an example of the body running the show.

We Have the Power to Change

These emotions create our moods, our temperament, and finally our personality. It is from this State of Mind that we make all of our decisions and respond to our life circumstances and to the people in our lives.

Through self-awareness, lots of introspection and a strong desire to make some positive changes in my life, I have curbed most of those self-defeating reactions. Now that I can recognize the pattern, I can catch myself before it catches me.

Do you often find yourself feeling frustrated, stressed worried, annoyed, impatient, resentful, angry, ashamed, guilty, fearful, cautious, sad, lonely or depressed? If these emotions outweigh the positive ones on a regular basis then the State of

Mind you are operating from can only bring back to you more of the same because our State of Mind is our individualized Energy Field, our frequency. (remember the Emotional Elevator?)

The good news is that we can change this. People make positive changes every day. Change begins with the awareness that you've been in an unhealthy pattern of behavior that you desire to change. This requires patience, determination, honesty and inspired action. Inspired action will move you forward, and step-by-step, you will feel the changes within you.

Not only are thoughts and emotions very powerful. But the worldwide medical community now believes that our emotional state directly impacts our physical health. This holistic view is the foundational belief of the integrative medicine movement.

The Mind-Body Connection

In his book, *Opening up: The Healing Power of Expressing Emotions,* J. Pennebaker mentions that even Sigmund Freud uncovered links between repressed emotions and physical symptoms nearly 100 years ago. Pennebaker and his colleagues demonstrated that those who repress their emotions simultaneously repress their immune system. When we hold on to anger or nurture grudges, jealousies, blame and assume a position of victim, we compromise our mental and physical health. Our bodies, through physical symptoms, are actually trying to tell us to pay attention.

In traditional Chinese medicine), emotions are considered the major cause of disease. Below is a list that shows how emotions affect our body:

Anger – weakens the immune system and damages the heart and liver.

Worry – affects digestion, the spleen, pancreas and the nervous system and can cause heart disease.

Stress – weakens the immune system, which promotes disease and affects brain and heart function.

Fear – can weaken the kidneys and bladder, and can affect our reproductive system.

Grief – can weaken the lungs, cause breathing problems and bowel disorders.

Depression – affects our colon and lungs.

Anxiety – affects the small intestine and the heart.

Love – brings peacefulness and harmony.

A Smile – brings happiness.

Looking at the above emotions and their associated physical manifestations, what physical symptoms do you experience? Refer back to the Emotional Elevator and the State of Mind you identified for yourself earlier, your signature vibration. Can you identify any emotions that could be compromising your health? Does this create an awareness for you about the nature of your well-being? Is there anything you may want to consider changing? Take some time to evaluate your emotional State of Mind and how it may be affecting your health.

Positive Emotions need to be acknowledged also. They can literally reverse the effects of negativity. Scientist, Barbara Fredrickson, claims that positive emotions can 1) broaden our perspective of the world, thus inspiring more creativity, wonder and 2) build over time, creating lasting emotional resilience. Fredrickson also claims that positive attitudes such as playfulness, awe, love, interest, serenity and feeling connected to others have a direct impact on health and well-being, and we can develop these ourselves with practice.

CHAPTER 7

The Power of a Smile

The emotion of a *smile* is fascinating, powerful and adds to our good health. In her book, *Smile, Happiness is Right Under Your Nose*, Mary Anne Puleio writes:

> *Do you think your smile is worth a million dollars? Your smile may be worth more than you realize. People who smile regularly have been shown to make more money, be more productive and have more job opportunities. Sincere smiles are a type of social currency that is valued by society. The sincerity of a person's smile can be seen as a sign of cooperation and trust and can weigh heavily on important decisions. A smile makes people more comfortable and well received. People equate smiles with acceptance. Scientists have found that as much as 75% of our opinion of others is influenced by non-verbal behavior, especially smiles.*

Physically, the act of smiling decreases stress and anxiety, relaxes our muscles, and improves respiration. It also increases mental and physical strength, and reduces pain. It is said that what you wear on your face is what you have in your body. Interestingly, these reactions can happen even if you fake a smile! As I've

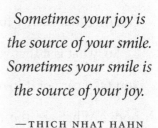

Sometimes your joy is the source of your smile. Sometimes your smile is the source of your joy.

—THICH NHAT HAHN

been saying for many years, if you put your mouth in a smiling position, a smiling feeling will follow. This all contributes to our health and well-being.

Happy Cells

The sole purpose of every cell in our body is to sustain our life and maintain good health in our body. All our cells work together as a team, twenty-four hours a day, seven days a week. We have about 100 trillion cells in our body, all under the command of our own thoughts, feelings and beliefs. This means that we are *totally in charge.* It also means that whatever we think, say and believe about our body, our cells believe also. And they respond accordingly, creating that reality for us.

So, what is it that you believe about your body? Do you take care of it lovingly? How do you talk to your body? What are the beliefs you carry around about your health or current conditions? Do you believe that you can take charge of your good health or have you resigned yourself to the belief that it's out of your control? Though I'm getting older, as we all are, I'm choosing to live young.

We've now learned that every cell in our body responds to every feeling we feel by releasing certain chemicals in our brain that affect our organs. When we feel good, when we are enjoying our life, when we look at the positive side of things, then we are making our cells happy. When our cells are happy, they can fully function to sustain our good health because they are filled with a strong *life force*.

On the other hand, when we are upset much of the time, then stress, tension and anxiety cause our cellular activity to slow down or even malfunction, and our chemical production is interrupted. Our breathing becomes shallow and our blood pressure goes up. If we experience these reactions in our body and mind on a regular basis, it interrupts the ability of our cells to maintain a healthy balance. This disturbance can then take the body out of ease and into dis-ease. As early as 400 BC, Socrates made this statement:

There is no disease of the body, apart from the mind.

Talk Love to Your Body

It's important to really appreciate your body, to be grateful every morning that you are alive and can appreciate all the beauty that life has to offer you. Hug yourself, feel your skin, savor the moment of communication with your body and thank your heart for never missing a beat.

If you have a particular ailment or condition in your body that needs healing, do not look at it with discouraging thoughts. Instead, interact with it, feel love for it. Tell it out loud, "I love you (foot) and I see and feel total health restored to you now and I am so grateful. Thank you." *Then listen to the message that it is giving you.*

You must believe it with all your being and keep smiling as you do this; it increases the frequency of the positive vibration. In order to make a difference you must make this a habitual thought pattern. (Just keep on remembering.)

The Power of the Present

Never project a desire as coming to you in the future, as in, "*Someday, I'll...*" because the future never comes. We are always in the *Now.* You have to love it into yourself. We can think about the past as a memory and think about the future, often with worry. But the only thing that's real is this *present moment.*

So, when you have a desire for better health you have to love it into yourself with positive vibrational thoughts, as if it's already here, and then say, *Thank you, thank you for my good health.* Do not allow any thoughts to the contrary. When they creep up, just say to yourself, *No thank you. I have all that I need. I claim perfect health for myself now.*

This also applies to your beliefs about aging and deterioration. Stop focusing on your chronological age and focus on feeling young. Stop noticing, stop listening, stop looking at anything that reinforces a belief in deterioration.

Honor Your Own Wisdom

Often, we get caught up in conversations about our aches and pains. Don't give in to it. You are the only one who can create your own reality. Don't follow someone else's version of it. Be your own person and be an example of joyful, positive thinking.

If you keep believing and hold on to a vision of yourself as you want to be and ignore the naysayers, you'll soon discover that you are feeling and looking wonderful. That's because *what you think about the most, is what you become.*

What's Your Frequency?

Some thoughts weaken us and some thoughts strengthen us. We've already learned about the electro-magnetic field of which we are all a part. We also know that the *frequency* of the vibration of our emotions attracts to us whatever is a vibratory match to our *frequency.* That can be good or bad. It all depends on the thoughts we are having, positive or negative.

It is very important to practice being aware of how we are feeling and what we are thinking and to become vigilant about catching ourselves in negativity. *Stop living unconsciously.* Put your feelings on a scale.

Through careful observation and by *paying attention*, try to determine how many of your thoughts, feelings, words, actions, and moods are positive versus negative. Can your positives tip the scale? Can they outweigh the negatives?

Embrace Optimism

When you decide to make a change, to move forward in your life, the only way you can open yourself up to, or create, that which you desire is by elevating your spirit, your frequency. You can't draw anything new or better to yourself by staying in the same mood. As Dr. Dispenza puts it, "You can't create a new future by holding on to the emotions of the past."

Optimism is the best medicine. So, keep smiling. Practice feeling good and before long you will discover that you no longer have to pretend to feel good.

Believe in yourself

*Believe in yourself, in the
power you have to control
your own life, day by day.
Believe in the strength you
have deep inside, and your
faith will show you the way.
Believe in tomorrow
and what it will bring,
let a hopeful heart
carry you through
For things will work out if you
trust and believe, there's no
limit to what you can do!*

That's when you will notice that things are beginning to change. You've tipped the scale! By the way, you only have to tip the scale to fifty-one percent to notice a positive difference.

It may not be easy at times, but in those times of struggle you will find a stronger sense of who you are, and you will also see yourself developing into the person you have always wanted to be.

Life is a journey through time, filled with many choices; each of us will experience life in our own special way. So when the days come that are filled with frustration and unexpected responsibilities; remember to believe in yourself and all you want your life to be, because challenges and changes will only help you to find strength and the dreams that you know are meant for you.

CHAPTER 8

The Neuroscience of Change

Your perspective is always limited by how much you know. Expand your knowledge and you will transform your mind.

—BRUCE LIPTON, PHD

For many years, scientists believed that our brain was hard-wired and totally developed by the time we reached early adulthood. They believed that once we were set in our ways we could not change our personalities, our habits and our beliefs. It was also strongly believed that we would eventually succumb to a predetermined, hereditary condition that one of our relatives had.

Many of us are still living with this mindset even though these beliefs are not true. Over the last forty to fifty years, advances in the study of neuroscience have disproven the above beliefs. The brain can and does change. It is constantly adapting to new surroundings, environments and new information. The brain's ability to change and adapt is called *neuroplasticity*.

The Brain

There are eighty-five billion nerve cells in our brain called neurons. These nerve cells communicate and connect with each other through electro-chemical circuits referred to as neurotransmitters or synaptic connections. This communication between the neurons leaves trails between them referred to as neural pathways.

We activate these neurons with every thought or memory we have. As the neurons are firing and wiring together through the circuits, they release chemicals into the body. As more thoughts come in, they are moved through neural pathways to unite with similar neurons. They eventually form clusters, or families, of neurons, which are activated by similar repetitive thoughts.

The more thoughts we have of a similar nature, the more clusters we create that wire together electrochemically. This forms deeper and stronger neural pathways and "easier accessibility" to more of the same thoughts.

The electro-chemical firing and wiring releases chemicals into our body, which create a stimulating effect. This can trigger addictive sensations, which we are not consciously aware of. These chemicals are actually emotions that infuse themselves into certain parts of the body to feel whatever emotion was signaled by the thought that generated it.

Mind-Body Connection

This is how the mind is always connecting with the body. *So, every time the mind has a thought, the body feels an emotion.* They work together as a team. If you have the same repetitive thoughts day after day, over long periods of time, you are then experiencing the same emotions day after day, over a long period of time. Eventually the brain gets stuck in these emotions and triggers behaviors, accordingly.

When you are living in repeated behaviors, they become your State of Mind and form your attitudes, disposition, and your personality. (Remember the Pattern of Being from Chapter 4.) If we are generally having happy, positive thoughts, then for the most part, our behaviors will not be self-destructive or self-defeating. If, however, our thoughts are filled with *poor me, not being good enough, everything is wrong with my life*, then our behaviors will demonstrate these thoughts with feelings of fear, anger, sadness, regret, grief, resentment, jealousy, etc. All this firing and wiring of thoughts and emotions create subtle addictive sensations in our body because of the chemicals released.

Cravings

Over a period of time our body begins to crave these sensations and will actually create emotional scenarios to duplicate those emotions. Once this happens, we've entered an addictive pattern and formed an *emotional comfort zone* and are now acting out self-sabotaging, self-defeating behaviors that we discussed in the Patterns of Being section in Chapter 4. (You may want to review them.) So, the body is now acting out behaviors without signals from the mind. The body has now taken over and has become the mind and the master.

This happens all too often and a classic example of this is food cravings. The mind does not instruct us to go to the refrigerator and get some ice cream. No, we get up off the couch in a semi-stupor and suddenly we find ourselves spooning ice cream into a large bowl. Almost all habitual thoughts, emotions and behaviors are performed in an unconscious manner. The times when our mind actually instructs our behavior, we are then, fully conscious of our actions and make conscious decisions. But when our body takes over, we are no longer in charge.

Who's Driving Your Life?

Have you ever driven home from work and as you pulled into your driveway you realize that you have no recollection of the drive home? So where were you and who was driving the car? Your mind was so preoccupied and maybe stressed about something that happened at work that you weren't paying attention. Luckily, your body already knew the way.

So much of the time we live our daily life in a habitual pattern of responses and reactions to the circumstances and people in our life, without consciously thinking

> *If you look at only what is, you might never attain what could be.*
>
> —UNKNOWN

things out. Sometimes we even look for things to be wrong because we need to experience that rush of adrenalin. Maybe because we are bored or depressed. Of course, we're not even aware that we are doing this. (Notice what you're noticing.)

This causes a great deal of drama in our life. Negative confrontations do come with a surge of adrenalin, but always make us feel defeated, disappointed in ourselves and heavy-hearted afterwards. This reinforces feelings of poor self-esteem. If it happens often, we can become discouraged about life in general, which can lead to depression.

CHAPTER 8

Creatures of Habit

Since most of the beliefs we live by were formed in our early childhood, then most of our thoughts, feelings and behaviors are based on those beliefs. This is what makes us creatures of habit. We all have our own unique traits and personalities and a way of responding to life situations. Thereby, it is our unique traits and personalities - formed by our beliefs, thoughts, feelings - that drive our behaviors and create the quality of our life. Take a look at your life and ask yourself:

Am I a generally happy person?

Am I doing the things that I find fulfilling?

Am I surrounded by the people I enjoy being with?

Do I feel financially secure?

Am I in a loving relationship?

Am I as healthy as I could be?

Am I generally enjoying my life?

If you answered no to any of those questions, then let's take a look at how *neuroplasticity*, the ability of the brain to change, can work in your favor.

Neuroplasticity

Whenever we are introduced to a new idea or concept or activity that piques our interest - like learning to dance, or play the piano, or play tennis, or speak a new language, or take a photography class, or join a gym, or visit a new country - we create new neural connections. This begins to change our brain. New activities generate new thoughts. New thoughts spawn new ideas.

Acting on new ideas opens a whole new world of possibilities, all the while creating more and more neural connections. The stimulation of new thoughts keeps the brain active and young. The more any new thoughts are repeated with emotion, the stronger that neural pathway becomes until the repetition of it becomes a habit.

The more open and willing we are to learn new things, the more we change our brain and the more exciting our life can be. Are you holding yourself back from trying something new? Have you convinced yourself that you just don't have the time or you're just too old to start something new? Sometimes just evaluating your life and setting new priorities can move you toward believing, "I'm worth this change and I'm going to go for it."

As you change the pictures in your mind, you are working to change the world outside your mind to fit the pictures.

—UNKNOWN

New activities stimulate the brain and elevate our mood by releasing "happy hormones." This is what *neuroplasticity* is about, the brain's ability to change itself. As the brain changes, we change. In fact, the best way to create a more fulfilling life is to simply be open to new ideas and points of view. Be willing to meet new people and try new experiences. What you may discover is that these new activities replace things you used to do because they are so much more fulfilling

Choosing to Dance Again

Let me share a story of a significant choice I made to change something. I grew up in an ethnic Ukrainian community where music and dance were a very big part of our cultural activities. I sang in a vocal ensemble, played a Ukrainian stringed instrument called a bandura and performed in an ethnic Ukrainian dance group. I don't know which I loved best, but I knew I loved to dance and move my body to music.

Although I was never allowed to go to any high school dances, I was encouraged to go to Zabavas. These were formal European-style dinner dances. They were adult events, but teenage girls were always welcome, escorted by family of course. Although I never felt I had enough outfits for school, my mother always sewed a proper ball gown for me to wear to a Zabava. This was important to her and I loved the music there, which was old European-style waltzes, rumbas, tangos and polkas, played by a wonderful live band. These were such glamorous events.

When we put our attention on something, we also take our attention off something else.

—DAVIDJI

The dance floor was always full, and all the gentlemen taught the young ladies how to dance properly. I especially loved the tango. I felt I had become a pretty good dancer and really enjoyed dancing anytime I had the opportunity.

Years later, while married to my first husband, we were invited to a wedding. When the music started, of course I wanted to dance. He wasn't interested so I got up and danced freestyle with many of the ladies on the floor.

When I returned to the table in a happy mood, he said to me, "You're a terrible dancer. You looked awful out there. You don't know how to dance." I was stunned and nearly started crying. I sat down in shock and didn't interact with anyone the rest of the evening. I felt embarrassed, like maybe it was true, maybe I did look ridiculous on the dance floor.

This was a man who completely intimidated me and I believed everything he said. (I know now that I allowed this.) I was so immobilized by that incident that I wouldn't dance for fifteen years. My heart ached every time I heard dance music, but I didn't have the courage to just get up and dance. I had lost all confidence in myself. "Emotional entrapment" literally keeps us immobilized in a cycle of unconscious behaviors that can keep us trapped in never changing circumstances.

My Leap of Faith

Fifteen years later while working on building up my confidence and self-esteem, I decided to take a leap of faith and go to a ballroom studio to learn how to dance. Deep inside me I knew I was a natural dancer, but I just couldn't trust that anymore. As I walked into the studio, I was scared to death and felt very insecure as if I had never danced before.

I will never forget my first group lesson. It was a Cha-Cha. I can't describe how exhilarating it made me feel to actually move my body to music for the first time in years. It was as if I had been injured and just learned to walk again. It almost made my heart explode. I was encouraged, complimented, acknowledged and I felt respected. I also became rather addicted to going to the dance studio and went at least five days a week for a while. It was like being starved for years and now I was feeding that hunger until I was satiated.

> *To dance is to be out of yourself, larger, more beautiful, more powerful. It is the glory on earth and it is yours for the taking.*
>
> —AGNES DE MILLE

The best part of taking that leap of faith to do something I loved again, after so many years, was the lasting friendships I made. I became part of a whole new community that I didn't even know existed. It literally changed my life in so many wonderful ways. I can't imagine how many neurons were wiring and firing in my brain through that experience. It definitely enhanced my well-being.

The Power of Choice

Just one new choice can have an amazing impact on your life. There are so many groups of people all around us who have special interests that we know nothing about simply because we haven't ventured out far enough to discover them. We haven't made the effort or we haven't given ourselves the permission to do so. (You know you want to.)

By nature, we really are creatures of community. One connection leads to another connection, leads to another connection and on and on. There is no end to the experiences that are available to us if we just take one step. So be your own hero, go ahead, venture out and take that leap of faith. Interaction with other like-minded individuals is incredibly uplifting and stimulating to our brain and our spirit. It truly enhances our whole being.

My desire for each one of you is that you will work to overcome your fears and make a choice that will open new doors, expand your horizons, build your self-esteem, put a smile on your face, and change your life dramatically.

Create Your Destiny

Watch your thoughts;

They become your words,

Watch your words;

They become your actions,

Watch your actions;

They become your habits,

Watch your habits;

They become your character,

Watch your character;

It becomes your

DESTINY.

CHAPTER 9

Preparing Your Mind for Change

We cannot become what we want
by remaining what we are.

—MAX DEPREE

Perhaps it's time to examine the life you've been living and check in to see how life has been treating you. Does something seem to be missing? Or maybe there is something you would like to remove from your life? Maybe you know exactly what it is, but just don't know how to go after it. How often have you said to yourself, *Okay, this time I'm really going to take care of this problem.* You take a few steps forward, and soon find yourself procrastinating again. What holds us back? What are we afraid of? Could lack of faith in ourselves, our abilities or a lack of self-worth be holding us back? Here is a list of some beliefs and negative thoughts that keep us from making a change toward living the life we dream about. These are all forms of the guilt, fear and shame that we discussed in Chapter 4. Let's review them:

Life always disappoints me.

I'll never be good enough.

I'm not meant to be successful.

I always feel left out.

People don't like me.

I'm always broke.

I'm not smart enough to compete with them.

I'll never get ahead.

I don't belong there anyway.

I never get chosen.

I just don't fit in.

Happiness is not for me.

What's the point?

Why bother?

I'm never going to make it anyway.

These are all manifestations of FEAR.

Sometimes, because we are functioning on auto pilot, we can be so detached from our inner self that we are hardly aware of the messages our mind is sending us. This self-defeating self-talk can be endless. How many of the above *false* beliefs have held you captive and prevented you from moving forward into a more fulfilling life? Most of these beliefs are rooted in a lack of self-love and worthiness. If you recall, earlier in this book I quoted Dennis Waitley, "It's not what you believe *you are* that holds you back, it's what you believe *you are not.*"

Change Behavior, Change the Brain

Outlining the neurological process of change, Dr. Joe Dispenza, best-selling author of *Breaking the Habit of Being Yourself,* explains that we are always moving from *thoughts* to *emotions* to *actions.* If we are open to it, the neo cortex, our *thinking brain,* allows us to learn new things from the environment around us as we take in knowledge through all our five senses. In the process, we build new neurons by creating new synaptic connections.

Old ways will not open new doors.

—UNKNOWN

The limbic brain is our *emotional brain.* It responds, emotionally to the thoughts going on in the neocortex. As we act on new information with corresponding emotions, we will find ourselves behaving differently. We are now creating new habits of thinking, feeling and doing. If we are no longer connecting to our old thoughts and behaviors, then their synaptic connections get smaller and smaller. If we never visit them again, they eventually disappear. These new experiences are creating new memories, stored in the cerebellum, the *memory center* of the brain. The memory center is now reminding us of our *new* thinking as we continue to reinforce our *new* behavior.

We are now in the process of *becoming someone new,* with new thoughts, new emotional responses, new behaviors and new experiences. We are also creating a new energy field. That's because we are now vibrating at a higher frequency and drawing to ourselves newer and more positive experiences.

Opening Up To Change

If you want to take a leap of faith right now, and you want to create a positive change in your life, start with love and compassion for *yourself.* Begin with knowing that you are worthy of your deepest longing and most cherished dreams. Embrace your worthiness with a strong willingness to move toward self-fulfillment. This willingness releases the resistance that holds you in a self-defeating mindset. Just be willing to take that first step. It's time to change those troubling circumstances and go for that dream to pursue your heart's desire. Let's take a look at how to move forward in that direction.

Change is Knocking

You see, change is always being offered to us; we're just not always sure how to approach it. Some change is initiated from outside of ourselves like being fired from a job, being asked to step into a new position, your spouse asking for a divorce, your boyfriend proposing, your house being foreclosed upon or winning the lottery. Life's circumstances bring us many opportunities to face change.

Most of us want to change for two reasons. We

either want to take something troubling out of our life or we want to add something new and exciting into it. For example, we may want to leave an abusive relationship. On the other hand, we may want to marry the love of our life. One is a takeaway and one is an addition. Both come from a desire for something better, and both require making a decision, and taking an action.

No movement towards change can be made without a decision. But it's in making the decision that all the self-defeating and limiting beliefs show up led by their leader, *fear*.

Feel the Fear

Fear is the opposite of faith and the enemy of joy, and it stops so many people from fulfilling their dreams.

Think about something that you've wanted to do for a long time, but for some reason, just haven't fully taken action on it. Then ask yourself, *Why? What is it that I've been afraid of? What kind of excuses have I been using?* Now ask yourself, *How would my life change if I could conquer these fears?* Visualize what it would look like and feel what it would feel like. Taking action toward our desires requires courage, and courage is simply overcoming fear, and fear is simply a feeling, which we sometimes let have great power over us.

Several years ago, author Ann Jeffers wrote a book entitled, *Feel the Fear and Do It Anyway.* Sometimes just acknowledging fear stops its power over us. Our awareness of it allows us to confront it. That increases our self-confidence and allows us to take charge. Every one of us has experienced fear; it's part of being human. Feeling fear now and then is normal until it becomes excessive and blocks our ability to happiness and success.

Making change requires determination, and a strong desire to change. Sometimes we vacillate for a long time before we take the first step. It has been said, *When the fear of things staying the same, exceeds the fear of making the change, that's when we take action.* Yes, change can often feel overwhelming, but you

> *It's kind of fun to do the impossible.*
>
> —WALT DISNEY

can make the shift as soon as that deep longing within you musters up enough courage to take action and make a commitment to yourself.

Studies have shown that the pleasure centers in our brain are activated as soon as we take the first step. That's because it gets us excited. We begin to anticipate the feeling and the reality of it as it gets closer. *Taking action empowers us; waiting keeps us a victim.* As soon as we take action towards the change we want, we get emotionally anchored to the desired result, and it moves us forward toward more inspired action.

CHAPTER 9

Courage

Brian Tracey, best-selling author and motivational speaker, tells us that there are three kinds of courage. First and most importantly is the *Courage to Begin,* to step out of our comfort zone in faith and trust to try something new.

The second kind of courage is the *Courage to Endure* and to stick with it once we have begun. It is persistence in the form of courageous patience to stand firm before we receive any kind of feedback or results from our actions.

The third kind of courage is the *Courage to Conquer Worry.* When we worry it is a form of *negative* goal setting. Instead of worrying, simply visualize a positive outcome and stay focused on this mental picture. Get in touch with the emotion you would feel when manifesting that vision.

Feel it Into Being

Change is an adventure and the journey begins in the mind. Best-selling author and inspirational speaker, Dr. Wayne Dyer, says it like this:

Assume the feeling of a wish fulfilled

You want to align yourself with the same energy as the object of your desire. As an example, how will it feel when you're driving your brand-new car? Close your eyes and vividly imagine opening the door for the first time, getting into your car and smelling that brand-new car smell, putting your hands on the steering wheel and the keys into the ignition. See yourself turn on the engine and feel the feeling of knowing, *this is my new car,* and then feel the feeling of driving it away.

You get the picture! This is how we create our desires. But because of our self-doubt and self-defeating habits, it's easy to become discouraged when attempting something new. Anxiety can set in and trigger loss of hope.

I firmly believe that the best place to start on this journey into transformation is to combat discouragement by *elevating your spirit*. You already know what I mean by this. Infuse yourself with *joy* so you can increase the frequency of your personal magnetic energy field. Then work yourself into a *smile*! This is a crucial component. Whatever it is that you desire, believe with all your heart that it has already arrived. You must feel it into your *Being* and into your *Now*! You must feel it into your life, with great love and gratitude. Have no doubt that it is already here, no matter how things may appear. *Your belief and your emotions must resonate together*. See through the eyes of the optimist, not the skeptic. You must have faith. Do this every day, minute by minute. Fake it until you make it with positive thoughts and actions.

Shift Your Mood!

Practice becoming aware of your fluctuating moods. As soon as a situation brings in a negative thought, diffuse it immediately. Say something like this, *I know this really irritates me, and I'm not going to give it power over me any longer. I will not let anyone or anything take away my joy. I'm in charge of my own thoughts and feelings and I know that everything is working well.* Just make a choice to hold on to your faith, and surround it with joy, no matter how things may appear.

The Wright Attitude

The Wright brothers changed history, but it was not an easy road. Here's how they kept believing. Whenever one of them would become discouraged because one of the steps failed, the other one would say, "It's all right, brother, because I can see myself riding in that machine, and it travels easily and steadily." The

Wright brothers had a dream they totally believed in, heart and soul. They knew what they wanted and kept that vision alive in their mind constantly. They were relentless in their faith, and their dream ultimately carried them through to build the first 'flying machine'. So, go ahead, create a detailed vision of your desire in your mind, follow through and keep on keeping on

Seminar leader, Mary Morrissey says, "You are not your circumstances." So, if you look around you and you don't like what you see, recognize that you are no longer a part of it. You have made an *energetic shift* in your mind, knowing that you will faithfully hold on to your dream until it has moved you right out of those circumstances.

> *Be ye transformed by the renewing of your mind.*
>
> —ROMANS 12:2

Strategies for Moving Through Change

It is important to be patient with yourself. This is all new and you are developing a whole new mindset, a new way of thinking that your brain is not used to. Doubts and even discouragement can set in. Make sure you recognize them. Don't negate them because *what you resist persists*. Calmly acknowledge them, accept them. Then take a deep breath and say to those doubts, *I know you want to come back, and I've already made my shift, so there is just no room for you here anymore.*

This is not about forcing a change. It's about moving through your ordinary daily routine with a big smile on your face knowing that you have a very special secret, *a secret that is transforming your life.* Hold on to that feeling and belief with all your heart. I use the word secret because it is important not to share your vision with others unless you know for sure that they are completely supportive. Others can often be discouraging. They have no attachment to your dream. (Remember the Cheesecake story?) Don't allow their opinion to alter your desires and change your uplifted energy.

Be a Pollyanna

When you are confronted with doubt, change your mental environment or your physical environment. Take a walk, get some fresh air, take a deep breath, smile, (don't get a snack), find a peaceful place to meditate. It's about, *not staying in negative vibrations* or emoting about a situation for hours. Practice letting go and switching gears. Do anything, or think of anything, that will make you feel good. Be a Pollyanna. Look at the world with rose-colored glasses. Reach for the way you would like to feel, even if it feels silly or stupid. It does take practice. *Do it anyway*! Make it a game. Laugh about it even if you feel cynical and don't believe it will work. *Do it anyway*! This doesn't mean you can't have both feet on the ground because you are doing this consciously now, not unconsciously.

Positive Momentum

The reason this is so important is because when you make yourself feel just a little better, the uplifted feeling will attract to you a higher sense of hopefulness. This new hopefulness will increase self-confidence and your belief in your ability to make a positive change. It will also increase your vibrational frequency, your *attractor factor*. That's inspired action! Without moving in this direction, discouragement can easily set in and stop you in your tracks.

> *You must find the place inside yourself, Where nothing is impossible.*
>
> —DEEPAK CHOPRA

So many of us succumb to discouragement and disbelief and never allow ourselves to fulfill our dreams. Don't let anything or anyone rob you of your most precious dreams and desires for a fulfilling and happy life. We all deserve to live our best life. So please, keep your frequency high!

If there is someTHING in your life that you truly have a desire to change at this time (it can't be a someONE) use the Cycle of Change pattern. This will allow you to stay focused, and monitor your emotions while moving forward to reach your goal.

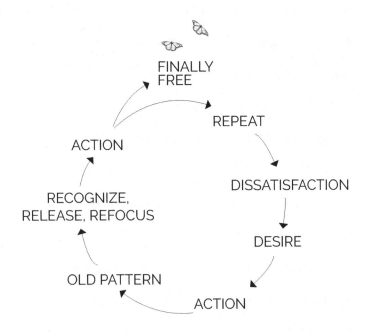

The Cycle of Change

1. **Dissatisfaction** is the first indication that you are troubled by something in your circumstances, usually on-going, that you have allowed to make you unhappy. It brings out feelings of sadness, anger, resentment, discouragement, or blame toward someone or something or toward yourself.

2. **Desire** happens when the dissatisfaction becomes uncomfortable enough that it leads to a desire for something better. We begin thinking of how we would like things to be and we envision a different outcome. Now we are dreaming of new possibilities and the steps needed to make a change.

3. **Action** involves creating a plan and stepping out into it. This step moves you out of your *comfort zone*. To feel the discomfort is your point of power. Don't fight it, recognize it and make it your friend.

It's just a feeling. Take a deep breath, *Feel the fear and Do it Anyway.*

4. **Back to the old pattern** is when you can't follow through because the fear is too overpowering, and you move right back into your comfort zone and back into your old patterns of behaviors.

5. **Recognize**, **release and refocus.** This is not a failure. It is a time to observe, evaluate, and recognize more clearly that the belief in the *fear* you have been carrying around is "just a feeling." It is not the truth, but it has been holding you hostage. With this awareness, you are now free to gently *release* it by saying, *"Good-bye, I no longer need you. You have no power over me and I release you now."* This gives you the freedom to take a breath and *refocus* on your *desire*. Visualize once more the fulfillment of your desire and feel the emotion of actually having it in your life right now.

6. **Back to action** with renewed inspiration you can now move forward into making your desire come true because fear is just a feeling that you can move beyond.

7. **If you fall a little short again, that's okay.** Maybe you got a little closer this time. Maybe it gave you some time to build up more courage. Have patience with yourself.

Don't beat yourself up! This might be a good time to stop for a *Moment of Gratitude* with a little prayer:

> *I didn't fail. I just found 10,000 ways it didn't work.*
>
> —THOMAS EDISON

"Thank you, God, for all I have and for helping me to keep on moving forward." Now simply go back to steps five and six and try again. Stay positive. Be kind. Just keep on keeping on until you succeed.

Enthusiasm

You can do anything if you have enthusiasm.
Enthusiasm is the yeast that makes your hope
rise to the stars. Enthusiasm is the sparkle in
your eye, it is the swing in your gait, the grip
of your hand, the irresistible surge of your
will and your energy to execute your ideas.
Enthusiasts are fighters. They have fortitude.
They have staying quality. Enthusiasm is at
the bottom of all progress.

With it there is accomplishment.
Without it there are only alibis.

—HENRY FORD I

Fall

HARVESTING HAPPINESS

*When summer's blooming has given its yield, we're
blessed by the harvested seeds of new direction.*

Time to reap the harvest of our growing
transformation, as the fruits of our labor shift from
self-defeat into clarity and freedom.

CHAPTER 10

Living on the Sunny Side

*Now and then it's good to pause in our
pursuit of happiness and just be happy.*

—UNKNOWN

Throughout history, humankind has been on a quest to find happiness, but we've always made it a struggle. We created the belief that happiness was about power, possessions, conquests - all things that only fed the ego. As civilization progressed, more and more became available to us, and we pursued all those things, outside of us, that we thought would bring us happiness. The desire in us for more created a need, which created ideas that manifested into new innovations, which led to more desires.

This is progress and it will always be, and it is a good thing. New technology has made our lives easier and healthier and safer. However, it has not necessarily made our lives happier. In our pursuit for more and better, we have become fixated and lost in a paradigm that tells us *we are not enough*. In trying to fill that void, we've neglected to feed our spirit, the only thing that can really bring us true happiness and fulfillment.

This void has now become obvious in our world and has spawned a growing consciousness, beginning with the holistic health movement to treat body-mind-spirit as one.

The Holistic Approach

The field of Energy Psychology from ancient eastern cultures has arrived on the scene in the west. It focuses on how our thoughts, emotions and behaviors relate to our biological energy system, and it uses a number of modalities to clear energetic blockages within our bio-field. Acupuncture is one of the most common in the west.

We have now come to understand that what we desire must first come from within us not from outside of us.

Very little is needed to make a happy life, it's in your way of thinking.

—MARCUS AURELIUS

Psychological and emotional well-being is being addressed today with meditation, emotional freedom technique (EFT, also known as Tapping), breath work, yoga, massage therapy, journaling, and numerous other therapies and modalities. These all work to quiet our emotions and elevate our spirit. It's the energy of an elevated spirit that fills us with true happiness.

The Finally Free Journey

Before we explore the many paths to happiness, let's take a closer look at what we've learned on this journey to be Finally Free and to create the life that we desire.

In The Prelude, we followed Portia Nelson as she struggled through her emotional journey of despair, from darkness into the light. She modeled for us how to finally free ourselves from the emotional entrapment of addictive behaviors and self-defeating belief.

In Chapter 1, we learned that we all live within the walls of a comfort zone of habitual behaviors created mostly by erroneous beliefs about how we fit in to the society around us.

Chapter 2 explained the interaction between the conscious and subconscious mind and how this forms our beliefs and our self-image.

Chapter 3 shared how childhood messages can profoundly influence our adult behaviors and beliefs for many years. You then wrote your own childhood story to discover the messages that impact your behaviors.

In **Chapter 4**, we explored the difference between life's two main motivators, Fear and Desire, and how they impact the way we face change in our lives. You were introduced to The Pattern of Being and learned how most of our self-defeating behaviors stem from guilt and fear.

In **Chapter 5**, we learned that we are all energetic beings living in an electro-magnetic field, and our thoughts and feelings create the reality we live in.

In **Chapter 6**, we were introduced to the Emotional Elevator, the range of emotions we feel as our vibrational thoughts fluctuate between positive and negative, and influence our moods, attitudes, and personality.

In **Chapter 7**, we discovered that every thought we have has a chemical reaction in our brain, creating an emotion that affects our body, vibrationally, in a positive or negative way.

Chapter 8 explained the neuroscience of change, and the process of neuroplasticity. We learned that we activate the neurons in our brain with every thought we have. If we repeatedly have the same thoughts, which trigger the same emotions, we will continue to live in repeated behaviors.

Chapter 9 took us through the process of making change with preparation and courage. We learned to feel the fear and do it anyway, to take a leap of faith, and follow the steps through the Cycle of Change.

This recap of the chapters reminds us that our human longing, even our deepest despair, is the result of our struggle between what we really desire for ourselves and what we believe we deserve. It's the battle between fear and desire.

Because fear comes in disguise from our subconscious programming, we often don't recognize it. But our actions can show us when we are operating out of fear. Have you ever made a decision that you knew wasn't in your best interest, yet you were compelled to do it anyway? We use lots of rationalizations when we do this, and allow our ego to take over.

Living in the feelings of our "distorted" thinking is a learned behavior that keeps us in the cycle of:

False Beliefs > Thoughts > Emotions > Behaviors

This erroneous pattern holds us back from all that is available to us. It blocks the confidence that would allow us to utilize all our talents, and it keeps us from fulfilling our heart's desire and from finding happiness. It's why so many of us settle for living mediocre lives.

Reflection

This book is about all of us. We're all on an emotional journey through life, searching for the secret that will release us from our struggles and for the road that will lead us to happiness and fulfillment.

So, as you were reading through the chapters, what was coming to mind? Did you identify with Portia Nelson's journey? Did you discover your comfort zones and were those discoveries AHA moments for you? Can you list the self-limiting beliefs that have blocked you from moving forward in your life? I recommend that you go through the chapters once again, jotting down what you learned about yourself from each chapter. Then ask yourself these questions and write out the answers:

What is the most significant thing that I discovered about myself from reading this book?

What has been my strongest characteristic?

What beliefs have been obstacles in my life?

What is my greatest desire?

Do I believe that I can fulfill it or will true happiness continue to elude me?

We Have the Power

In Chapter 5, we learned that the secret answer to all of our desires is all around us and within us. We are powerful energetic beings who are able to control our thoughts and feelings because we live in an electromagnetic field. Once we understand the dynamics of how this all works, we no longer need to be victims of our subconscious mind. We simply have to open our mind to recognize the power that we truly have available to us.

We can now decide what life we want to live, and feel that we deserve everything we desire. This may require a major shift in our belief system and the way we think and feel about things. It may feel like you are thinking backwards. But if you follow through, your life can change dramatically. Let's review three basic principles:

1. We are electromagnetic beings living in an electromagnetic universe and everything in

our life is controlled by how we interact with this field.

2. We interact with it through the vibrations of our thoughts, of our feelings, and of the words we speak.

3. We attract to us exactly what we've been thinking, how we've been feeling, and what we've been saying to ourselves and to others.

How We Project Our Energy

Everything we say, do and feel carries a vibration. Many of these are unconscious, habitual actions that we pay very little attention to. Yet, they are sending out a signal about us that others pick up. In order for us to take charge of where our life is going, we must become exceedingly aware of what kind of energy we are projecting. The general mood we are in most of the time, our vibrational set point, has been our *attractor factor* in our life. Pay attention to the following questions. How would you answer them?

Are you aware of your mood most of the time?

What tone do you use when you interact with family members, your spouse, your children work associates, friends, store personnel, etc.?

What expression do you carry on your face, most of the time? Is it pleasant, serious, stern, angry, moody, or happy?

Do you greet people on the street, make eye contact, smile or ignore them?

How do you carry your body? Do you walk with a lively sprint or drag yourself around with slumped shoulders?

How often do you smile?

All of this expresses our vibration and brings back to us circumstances that match it.

Creating a New Reality

If we truly want a better life, then we must pay attention! We must create an awareness about all of our actions, thoughts and feelings. We need to be vigilant about our general mood and make a habit of noticing the good things. Eventually, the "not so good things" have a way of working themselves out.

Awareness can help us catch ourselves when we're about to lose our tempers, Smile even if we have to fake it until we make it. We're practicing! We are learning to be *happy*. You see, by creating a new reality in your mind and focusing on that picture you can slowly release your attachment to the old reality, if that is what you desire.

Most importantly, however, we must stop focusing on that which does not bring us joy. We can also recognize our reactions and ask ourselves: *Why is this a good thing?* When we can find the blessing in the challenges, we can shift our experience. This might take a little practice. Have patience with yourself and keep using these tools.

If we want to draw positive things into our lives, we must first vibrate as positive people. Staying in a positive mood opens us up to receiving solutions to problems. We must believe in our dreams by envisioning and feeling

The future belongs to those who believe in the beauty of their dreams.

—ELEANOR ROOSEVELT

the emotion of already having them in our life right now because NOW is the only time there is. Feel the presence of them all around you.

We must feel it into being - no doubts. Our vibration must resonate with that which we desire. Verbally affirm how wonderful it feels now that our dream is right before our eyes! As Greek author and philosopher, Nikos Kazantzakis, expressed, "The non-existent is whatever we have not sufficiently desired."

Elevating Our Spirit

Many of us complain that our everyday life experiences and circumstances are often stressful and discouraging. The responsibilities that pull us in different directions cause anxiety and make us long for something better. However, if all we do is long for something better, we're really sending out the message of "what we don't have" rather than "what we desire." Whatever circumstances we want to change can only be done from the inside. As Dr. Wayne Dyer used to say, "If you change the way you look at things, the things you look at change."

You can't force change from the outside, but you can plant seeds of a new vision and then embrace the feeling of them consistently, not just now and then.

Doing anything that makes us feel good is the key that will keep us moving closer and closer to our desire. It's about elevating our spirit by finding activities that support the feeling of happiness and well-being.

Activities that will fill our minds with positive hopeful thoughts can replace old discouraging ones. Once we discover activities that fill our hearts with joy, we must make them on-going habits. By constantly feeding our spirit with uplifting thoughts and emotions, we will be consistently drawing to us that which we desire.

Choose from anything you love doing. It can be as simple as taking a walk every day or setting aside a specific time to read or journal or play with your pet or create a photo album or just enjoy a magazine without feeling guilty. If all you have is fifteen minutes a day, just make it consistent. You'll soon find that fifteen minutes can turn into twenty minutes. Pamper yourself with LOVE and embrace your worthiness.

Micro-Meditation

Before we move forward, let's stop, take a deep breath, close our eyes and honor who and where we are right now on life's journey. Let's feel appreciation for all that life has shown us, and how we have grown through our experiences. We are now ready to embark on the next leg of life's journey, bringing with us our newfound belief in our self, knowing that we are worthy of our heart's desires. So, imagine where we want to be. Re-imagine ourselves and our circumstances. See them in full detail and feel the exhilaration of being there. Carry that vision and emotion with us everywhere and keep smiling because we know that it is already here!

The following tools will help us make these dreams come true because they direct our energy and keep our spirits high. Their goal is to reprogram our subconscious beliefs about what is possible for us. They work through consistent repetition and by infusing our emotions with a newfound belief and inspiration. Repeat for at least thirty days in order to activate the reprogramming.

Visualization

This is a daily, intentional practice of visualizing in our mind a scenario of an outcome we desire. It is creation through visualization. What we can see with our mind, we can manifest in the physical. For the best results, follow these guidelines:

1. Set aside ten minutes twice a day to sit quietly with our eyes closed and envision the most perfect picture of our desire.

2. Create a detailed very specific and clear picture.

3. See ourselves in the picture enjoying it all now.

4. Feel the joyful, exciting emotions of being there.

5. Engage our senses of sound, smell, taste, feel.

6. Do this for at least thirty days, consistently.

Affirmations, Positive Self-talk

This uses positive, affirmative statements to create a desired outcome in a situation.

For best results, follow these guidelines:

1. Write out clear, specific statements about how we would like something to be.

2. Be positive.

3. Use strong, exciting adverbs and adjectives.

4. Keep the statement in the present tense to show it is happening NOW. Instead of, *I'm going to lose weight,* say, *I'm losing weight now.*

5. Use *I am* instead of *I will.*

6. Do not use *I want*; it expresses, *I don't have.*

7. The more specific, the stronger the impact.

8. After we've written out our affirmations, begin reading them out loud, with emotion and do this every day for at least thirty days. We can even post them on our walls or mirror.

Examples of Positive Affirmations

I am a beautiful person.

Self-confidence is evident in all that I do.

I'm so grateful for my wonderful job.

I'm so excited about my unfolding future.

I'm so grateful for the support of my family.

I'm strong, capable and determined.

Life is so good to me.

I attract prosperity of every kind.

My home is filled with peace and harmony.

Gratitude: Affirmation of Good in the World

Feeling and acting out in genuine gratitude has an amazing effect on uplifting our vibrational energy, and boosting our physical and mental health.

According to Dr. Joseph Mercola, studies show that a state of gratitude has benefits on every organ system in the body. It improves our heart health, reduces stress, and regulates our mood by activating our neurotransmitters, serotonin and dopamine levels. We can enhance our general sense of well-being by practicing an attitude of gratitude.

Something as simple as noticing a pleasant smell, seeing our flag waiving in the wind, feeling the cool breeze through your hair, hearing a young child's giggle, all bring a sense of well-being. Remembering to express our pleasure out loud for all these delightful little things will keep our mind off all the other stuff. There is a world of opportunities to show our gratitude and every time we do, we reap the benefit of knowing we did something good. So, acknowledge others often with thanks, hugs and smiles.

One of the most beneficial habits is to use a daily Gratitude Journal. The regular practice of finding peaceful moments, reflecting on our feelings of appreciation, and writing them down allows us to connect with the healing power of gratitude. There are so many benefits to this practice. It can help us gain a better perspective on what's really important in our life, and help us learn more about ourselves. When we're feeling a little down, reading through it can really lift our spirits.

Forgiveness

Forgiveness is finally arriving into the State of Mind that allows us let go of the hurt, anger and the resentment of being wronged. It is a choice to let go of the burden of bitterness and a desire to retaliate or punish. It's giving up the poisons of blame and hatred. Holding on to resentment, anger and blame holds us in debilitating energy that disempowers us. Forgiveness can:

- Renew relationships

- Renew trust

- Bring resolution

- Dissolve the pain of the past

- Create a brighter future.

We just explored a number of activities that can elevate our vibrations. It's about living in a consciousness of high vibrations that allows us to attract the life that we desire. There are endless ways to do this, and we covered just a few. They can move you forward if you use them conscientiously and consistently.

Release to Embrace Self-love

Our power to change our circumstances and reshape our lives begins with our willingness to look within and search for the places where we are not feeling self-love. Take a deep look within and recognize that you, yourself, are a perfect creation created in love. Love only sees **good** in you. So, in all your perceived imperfections, you are still perfect. Embrace your worthiness and feel your self-love expand to all others and release all that does not feel good.

It is that wounded, unforgetting part of us that makes forgiveness an act of compassion rather than one of simple forgetting.

—DAVID WHYTE

In releasing the thoughts and beliefs that no longer serve you, feel the heaviness of those burdens disappear. Inhale the freshness and joy as you anticipate the wonderful new things to come. You are now ready to bring to mind, with clarity, that which you desire. Bring yourself into this space as often as possible, accepting nothing contradictory and watch your life transform.

CHAPTER 11

Who Am I and Where Have I Been?

Self-Awareness is a fundamental principle in changing your mindset and loving yourself.

—DR. ANDREA PENNINGTON

In the previous chapters, we explored the process of change. We examined the neurological process, the role of fear, and the actual steps to making a change. Now we're going to examine who we have been and where we are at this moment. In order to move forward in any direction, you have to know your starting point

- who you are now and where you've been - and what you really desire. So, in this chapter we're going to take a journey into self-discovery to set the foundation for creating the life of your dreams.

Through a series of self-evaluation exercises, you will gain more clarity into many aspects of yourself that you may not have explored before. Learning who you are, through an honest self-assessment, and accepting the truth of your discoveries, enables you to rise above and move forward into personal transformation. By putting all the broken pieces together, you can move into a new and more authentic version of yourself.

The first series of exercises will give you the opportunity to pause and really think about yourself, something most of us rarely do. It is important to begin recognizing and acknowledging some of your qualities. This is a starting point for self-evaluation.

How Many Describe You?

In this checklist, circle all the words that describe you.

Academic	Dependable	Intelligent	Rational
Active	Determined	Kind	Realistic
Adaptable	Dignified	Leisurely	Reasonable
Adventurous	Discreet	Lighthearted	Reflective
Affectionate	Dominant	Likable	Relaxed
Aggressive	Eager	Logical	Reserved
Alert	Easygoing	Loyal	Resourceful
Ambitious	Efficient	Mature	Responsible
Artistic	Emotional	Methodical	Robust
Assertive	Energetic	Meticulous	Self-confident
Bold	Enterprising	Modest	Self-controlled
Broadminded	Enthusiastic	Obliging	Sensible
Businesslike	Fair-minded	Open-minded	Sensitive
Calm	Farsighted	Opportunistic	Serious
Capable	Firm	Optimistic	Sharp-witted
Careful	Flexible	Organized	Sincere
Cautious	Forceful	Original	Sociable

Charming	Formal	Outgoing	Spontaneous
Cheerful	Frank	Patient	Spunky
Clear thinker	Friendly	Peaceful	Stable
Clever	Generous	Persevering	Steady
Competent	Gentle	Pleasant	Strong
Competitive	Good-natured	Poised	Strong-minded
Confiden	Healthy	Polite	Sympathetic
Conscientious	Helpful	Practical	Tactful
Conservative	Honest	Precise	Teachable
Cool	Humorous	Progressive	Tenacious
Cooperative	Idealistic	Prudent	Thorough
Courageous	Imaginative	Purposeful	Thoughtful
Creative	Independent	Painstaking	Tolerant
Curious	Industrious	Quick	Trusting
Unassuming	Understanding	Unexcitable	Uninhibited
Verbal	Versatile	Warm	Wholesome
Wise	Witty	Zany	

Now go over the list again and put a check mark next to the words that you feel are your strongest attributes You've now discovered many of your strengths. That is a good thing. Stay aware of them, feel good about them, make them part of your self-image.

Now, go over the list again and look at those you did not choose. Underline any quality that you feel you would like to possess. For example, you might think, *"Perhaps I should try to be more tactful when I'm speaking with others."* or *"It would be good for me to be more outgoing."* These are some of the steps to becoming more of who you really want to be. Below, list the qualities that you identified as your most important strengths so you can easily refer to them.

*Don't judge each day by the harvest
that you reap, but by the seeds
that you planted.*

—ROBERT L. STEVENSON

Self-Evaluation of Personal Qualities

Evaluate yourself on each quality below by using the following scale: put the number value to the right of the quality and circle the number.

1-Nearly perfect	5-Below Average
2-Good	6-Deficient
3-Above Average	7-Almost completely lacking
4-Average	

Physical qualities		Mental Qualities	
Vitality		Quickness of thought	
General good health		Imagination	
Good posture		Good memory	
Pleasing facial expression		Concentration	
Personal neatness		Sound judgement	
Dressing appropriately		Resourcefulness	
Control of body (sit quietly)		Ability to speak well	
Organized		Attention to detail	
Punctual		Fair-minded	

Tempermental/Emotional Qualities

Evaluate yourself on each quality below by using the 1-7 scale above. Put the number value to the right of the quality and circle the number.

Courtesy		Courage	
Tact		Ambition	
Truthfulness		Sincerity	
Integrity		Cheerfulness	
Loyalty		Poise	
Enthusiasm		Helpfulness	
Self-control		Initiative	
Self-confidence		Open to suggestions	
Stability		Persuasiveness	

1. Which five qualities are you most happy with?

2. Which five qualities would you like to improve?

3. What steps can you take to improve these?

Eight Important Areas of Life

Now, let's take a look at eight different areas of your life. This will require more thoughtfulness and introspection. Take some time doing this even if you have to put it down for a while and come back to it.

Directions: On eight separate sheets of paper label one category at the top of each page. Answer the four questions below for each of the categories. Write the question before you answer it.

Family	What's working in this area?
Career	
Health	What's not working in this area?
Self-Improvement	
Financial	How would you like it to change?
Social	
Spiritual	What steps can you take to change it?
Material Desires	

Review the exercise you just completed then answer the questions below.

In which of the areas are you most satisfied? Which area are you most concerned with? Are you willing to take action to change in this area? How will making a change in this area benefit you? What's the most significant thing that you learned about yourself doing the last exercise? What did you discover? Does something in particular stand out in your mind? Write about it in detail.

Unearthing Your Past

In this next section, you will explore the memories of your past as far back as your ancestors. In your mind, you will explore stories you were told, conversations you overheard, attitudes that were expressed, situations that you witnessed, the feelings that you felt, and the beliefs that you came away with.

In the following set of exercises, you will begin to identify your self-limiting subconscious beliefs from your childhood. You will also recognize your positive qualities that were also established in your childhood. These are the beliefs that built your self-concept and who you are today. Unearthing and bringing them to the surface of your awareness will allow you to "consciously" examine them so they are no longer hidden in your subconscious mind. Until we actually learn the nature of our programming, we will not recognize how our behavior is being influenced by it.

While answering the questions in this section you will experience several AHA moments and may even find yourself needing to take a deep breath while expressing, *"Wow! I never realized that about myself."* This is truly a self-discovery and evaluation process.

To experience it successfully, I recommend you take several days to go through it. There is no need to rush. Don't just answer the question. Feel through it and visualize your answer. Try to connect with the emotions of that experience and keep on writing as long as the answer is flowing. Very often, as you are processing this experience, many other emotions come up along with the memories associated with them. When this happens, on a separate piece of paper, jot down the memory and the emotion immediately. A fleeting memory can disappear as quickly as it showed up. I know this from experience.

You may also find that you can't stop writing about that experience because more and more memories keep coming to the surface. Don't stop. This is very therapeutic. You're probably releasing long held emotions that you have been, unknowingly, acting out for a long time.

This is your self-discovery time. I recommend that you use a separate notebook for this experience. Before you begin, make sure you are in a quiet place where you won't be disturbed. Take several deep breaths, relax and begin.

Examining Your Roots

What do you know about your ancestors and your heritage? You may have heard stories about them from your grandparents or other relatives. To the best of your memory, answer the following questions:

What did they live through historically?

What great struggles did they encounter?

Which religious principles did they follow?

Were they generally happy people?

Did they work hard for their family?

Were they loving and compassionate?

What kind of impressions were you left with?

Do you feel you adopted some of their values or beliefs?

Is there a particular relative who is talked about in your family and why?

What in your life has been carried down to you through their experiences?

How do you feel about your heritage?

Do you carry a sense of pride about your ancestors or are you uncomfortable with them?

If you could choose another life, would you choose who you are now or would you change your nationality, your sex or your race?

What did you discover about yourself?

Your Maternal Grandparents

(If you did not know them, just say that.)

What was your relationship like with them?

Were they loving and warm or formal and indifferent?

Did you feel loved by them?

Did you feel safe with them?

How much did they interact with you?

Did you have fun when you were with them?

How often did you see them?

What did you learn from them?

What's your favorite memory of them?

What's your worst memory of them?

Your Paternal Grandparents

Answer the same questions as for maternal grandparents.

What did you discover about yourself?

Your Mother

What was she like?

Was she warm and loving or strict and unaffectionate?

What did your mother often say to you?

What is your favorite memory of her?

What is your worst memory of her?

What was your mother's main advice?

What did she want you to be and why?

What did you enjoy doing with your mother?

Did she encourage you or show disapproval?

Were you ever afraid of your mother?

How did you feel about yourself in her company?

Your Father

Answer the same questions as for your mother.

What did you discover about yourself?

Your Relationship with your Siblings

How many siblings did you have and what was the age difference between you and them?

Did you get along well?

Did you enjoy each other and play together well?

Was there rivalry and competition between you?

Did you fight with each other?

Were you generally happy to be with them?

Did they ever pick on you?

Did you ever feel left out?

Did you ever feel that your siblings were favored more by your parents or grandparents?

Did you feel confident when with your siblings?

What was your worst experience with one or more of your siblings?

What was your favorite game?

Did you have a favorite sibling?

Did you ever share secrets with one and not the others?

Did one or more of you ever gang up on another?

What was your favorite memory of your siblings?

What word describes your relationship with them?

What have you discovered about yourself?

General Childhood Memories

What were your earliest childhood memories?

What was your happiest childhood memory?

What was your favorite childhood story, fairytale, book, hero, movie or TV program?

What did you want to be when you grew up?

Did you have a nickname when you were young?

Did you like school?

Did you have lots of friends or were you a loner?

What kind of student were you?

When you were little, what did the family talk about at dinner?

As a young child, did you experience any difficult, challenging or even traumatic moments? Did they color your beliefs about life as an adult?

As a young child, did you experience any serious health challenges. If so, how did this affect your attitudes today?

Do any memories of your childhood haunt you today?

What did you believe about yourself as a child?

What did you discover about yourself?

Your Teenage Years

Describe yourself as a teenager.

What were you concerned about?

How were you emotionally?

What were your favorite activities?

Did you feel confident or insecure?

How was your experience at school?

What was your favorite class?

What was your worst class?

Were you a joiner or a loner?

What did you want to be when you grew up?

Did you have strong career aspirations?

How was your relationship with your parents?

Were they supportive or always challenging you?

Did they give you lots of responsibilities?

Were you generally happy?

What were your happiest memories as a teenager?

Did you ever get into serious trouble?

Did you date as a teenager? Was that a good experience?

Did you enjoy reading? What were your favorite books, movies, music?

What was your biggest challenge as a teenager? How did this impact your beliefs today?

What is your worst memory as a teenager?

What values and beliefs did you pick up about yourself
at this time?

What did you discover about yourself?

Your Young Adult Life (in your 20s)

What did you do after high school - college, trade
school, job?

Where did you live? Did you like where you lived?

What kind of social live did you have?

Who were the important people in your life?

How did you feel about yourself - confident or
insecure?

How do you think you were regarded by your peers?

Did you date? Did you have a special love interest?

What major decisions did you make at this time?

What beliefs and values determined the decisions at
that time?

Do you have any major regrets about the choices you
made at that time?

What would you have done differently?

What are you most proud of during this time?

What did you discover about yourself?

Your Adult Life

Career

What has your career life been like - positive, rewarding or full of struggles?

How have your beliefs about your abilities affected your career choices?

Do you love what you are doing?

Are you looking for a change?

What career would you really love?

If you are seeking change, can you identify which beliefs about yourself have been holding you back?

Is there something specific in your life that you feel is a real obstacle to move forward with a plan?

Are you ready to take the steps to change?

Finances

Describe your financial history. How has your financial history influenced your self-esteem?

Do you believe you are financially successful?

Have finances been a struggle for you?

What beliefs about money come from your parents?

What did they teach you about spending money?

Were you parents financially successful or was money a struggle for them?

Was your father a spender or saver?

Was your mother a spender or saver?

Who do you believe influenced you the most regarding your money habits?

Are you a spender or saver?

What do you spend your money on?

What beliefs do you hold onto that may be an obstacle to your financial success?

Are you willing to begin letting them go?

Relationships

Who has most significantly influenced your life in a positive way?

How have you grown/changed as a result?

What qualities do you admire about him/her?

Do you try to emulate those characteristics?

What opinions do others have of you?

How does their opinion influence your decisions?

Do you have friends who support and believe in you?

Who is the most important person in your life?

Who has been the most difficult and troublesome person in your life?

How was your life affected by him/her?

Are there any relationships that need healing or forgiveness in your life? Are you ready to do that?

Through the Years

What have you learned about yourself throughout your lifetime?

Have there been recurring themes, situations that seem to happen over and over?

Have you found yourself continuously having the same emotional responses to life situations?

Who was always there for you, no matter what?

Who inspired you to keep moving forward?

How have you changed since your teenage years?

Final Reflection Questions

What have you discovered about yourself while doing these self-evaluation exercises?

Has it been insightful?

Did you discover things you were not aware of before?

What was the biggest surprise?

Was there anything that disappointed you?

What inspired you and made you feel hopeful?

Are you excited to begin a new journey into your transformation to build a more fulfilling life?

Congratulations, you've just completed an enormous amount of introspection! Give yourself a few days to process and internalize the information. While your brain is processing all these new insights, jot down any thoughts or ideas that come into your head and any emotions that are triggered because they may disappear. You may feel overwhelmed by it all and say to yourself, *Now what do I do?* or you may know exactly what you want to do because of the insights and AHA moments that you experienced.

As you continue to process all that you've learned about yourself you will gain more clarity and begin to focus on what you really desire in your life. Now that you've thoroughly examined your past, you have the awareness to release the beliefs and behaviors that have not served you well and to create a more empowering story. This is the time to ask yourself, *What kind of life do I really want to live? What do I want it to look like?"* Find a quiet moment, relax, close your eyes and begin to daydream about how your new life will look.

Your New Life

In order to start creating the life of your dreams, you need to be clear on exactly what you want. The best way to begin is to categorize your life into segments and focus on each one at a time. Your answers will come from all the information you just absorbed. You can start with the following categories and then add any others that may apply to you: **Relationships, Home life, Spouse, Children, Relatives, Health, Career life, Money/Finances, Social life, Friendships, Creative life, Recreation, Romance,** etc.

It is also helpful to breakdown your categories into other segments as they apply to your life. The more you can break your thoughts down, the more clarity you can create about what specifically you desire. This really helps when you are visualizing "your dream life."

Write it Down

Now that you've categorized your hopes and dreams, it's time to put them in writing. Go category by category, in any order. Simply list the category and next to it write what you would like it to be. For example:

Relationship: *I'd like to build a stronger deeper relationship with my spouse by spending more time traveling together.*

Whatever is drawing you into a particular area is probably the best place to start. You can add as many desires as you like into each category. As you begin each category, ask yourself, *What do I really want here?* This may be a lengthy exercise, but going through it is like living through it, which will put you in vibratory connection with your desires. **This is the most important purpose of this process.** So, stay emotionally connected to your writing because your emotions carry the vibrations that will draw to you exactly what you want. Don't make this a project; make it an experience. It's not about how fast you can finish. The longer you stay with it the stronger your vibrations will become. Now begin writing!

Feel it Growing

Congratulations once more! You have planted the seeds! This has probably been an emotional, self-acknowledging and enlightening experience. It has elevated your spirit and has brought you energetically closer to your desires. Take a break now, relax and leave it alone for a day or two and let your mind process what you have been writing. Let the seeds you have planted grow. The energy of this will stay with you because you won't be able to stop thinking about it. When you come back to it, re-read it again and this time relax, breathe, and really let yourself go into a deep dream state or meditation while visualizing how your new and exciting life looks and what it feels like at this moment, now, in the present. Watch your new life grow and bloom.

You are now ready to write your *New Life Story,* *which you will be creating and living by following the* *guidelines below.*

Guidelines For Your New Life Story

Write your story in the present tense, as if it were happening right now. Now is the only time your subconscious lives in.

All statements must be positive. Remember, you are writing the way you want it to be. Be descriptive, detailed, colorful, specific and exciting.

Describe how good these new things and experiences are now making you feel by adding your feelings and emotions into the picture.

Make sure you keep yourself in the picture by

visualizing yourself in the new experience with a big smile on your face.

Feel Your Worthiness. Do not negate this experience with any thoughts like, Oh, I'm probably asking for too much. There is no such thing as, "Too Much" for the universe, unless that is your belief.

Once you have completed writing your *New Life Story,* the next step is to read it out loud to yourself, twice daily with enthusiasm and unquestionable expectation, feeling every word and visualizing every scenario for at least thirty consecutive days to get the vibrations activated. I suggest you continue reading your story out loud once a week to keep the excitement fresh in your consciousness. You must "joyfully" resonate with that which you desire. It's all about your energy, and it's your emotions that carry the vibrations that cause creation. Act as if you are already living your new life. You will slowly feel the uplifting of your energy as you watch your life transform.

In Closing

In conclusion, I want to leave you with the notion that life is a creative process and **you are the creator of your life.** Your life is a piece of art - a panorama, a landscape, or a self-portrait. You have all the tools and all the colors of the universe to inspire you. Whatever it is that you desire, you can "make it happen" by simply painting your desires on the canvas of your life. And finally: *Hold on to the vision and energy of your dreams until what you see in your mind becomes what you see with your eyes.*

Suggested Reading List

Assaraf, John. *Innercise.*

Atkinson, William Walker. *Thought Vibration.*

Braden, Gregg. *The Divine Matrix.*

Brown, Brene. *Rising Strong.*

Byrne, Rhonda. *The Power.*

Church, Dawson. *Mind to Matter.*

Dispenza, Dr. Joe. *Becoming Supernatural.*

Dooley, Mike. *Manifesting Change.*

Dyer, Dr. Wayne. *I Can See Clearly Now.*

Grabhorn, Lynn. *Excuse Me, Your Life Is Waiting.*

Grout, Pam. *E-Squared.*

Harris, Bill. *Thresholds of the Mind.*

Hawkins, Dr. David R. *Power vs Force.*

Hay, Louise. *You Can Heal Your Life.*

Hicks, Esther and Jerry. *Ask and It Is Given.*

Hill, Napoleon. *Think and Grow Rich.*

Jampolsky, Gerald G. *Love is Letting Go of Fear.*

Lipton Ph.D., Bruce H. *Biology of Belief.*

Munroe, Dr. Myles. *Principles and Power of Vision.*

Nicholson, Ester. *Soul Recovery.*

Puleio, Mary Anne, Ph.D *Smile.*

Rubin, Gretchen. *The Happiness Project.*

Scovel Shinn, Florence. *The Wisdom of Florence Scovel Shinn*

Vanzant, Iyanla. *Forgiveness.*

Vitale, Dr. Joe. *The Attractor Factor.*

Waitley. Dennis D. *The Psychology of Winning.*

Wilde, Stuart. *The Force.*

Valentina's Story

The one constant picture that I have carried throughout my life has been of me as a teacher. And so, while writing this book, I envisioned myself standing in front of my classroom, looking into the eyes of my students, hoping that my words would touch their hearts and minds and make a positive impact on their lives.

As my readers, you, too, have been like my students. I shared with you the insights that I have gained from my life journey and the choices I made along the way. Here I would like to share with you the experiences of my early childhood. Being a cautious learner gave me more time to process my traumatic early childhood. My perceived abandonment and kidnapping left me with deep emotional scars, fears and insecurities.

For nearly a year when I was three years old, I did not know where I was or who I was with. I was taken away from my home and brought to a strange and frightening place by a couple I did not know. I was scared and did not know what was happening to me. To add to my fear and confusion, the people around me were speaking a language I did not understand.

Although everyone there seemed to be kind to me, I never knew if I was safe. Since I could neither understand nor communicate, I stayed silent, but my eyes and ears were always on guard. I was scared all of the time, but due to that fear I expressed no emotion. I became an observer, instead. Always on guard, I watched people intensely, never knowing if someone else was going to take me away.

I learned to distinguish facial expressions, pitch and tonality of voice, and the way people moved and carried their bodies. I was always trying to perceive what people were thinking (I still do). I knew it all meant something. But it was the eyes that revealed to me the depth of their sorrow and the nature of their character. I knew this intuitively. In my silence, I learned to tune into their emotions and my little four-year-old heart began to develop compassion.

I soon learned to understand and then speak my new language. In doing so, some of my fear was released and I became more and more comfortable with my new surroundings and the couple who had "kidnapped" me. Because they were kind, loving, and protective, I began developing a sense of trust and safety with them. It turned out that they were really my parents and we were in a Ukrainian Displaced Person's camp (DP) in Germany after the Second World War.

I, however, had been living with a German family who took care of me at a time when my parents could not. I always believed they were my true family and I knew that they genuinely loved me. I desperately missed them and my lovely little cottage home in the mountains where everything was so peaceful and where I was so happy. I could not understand why they were not coming to get me. How could they let this happen to me? I felt so lost and abandoned. Did I do something wrong and they didn't want me anymore? Maybe they really didn't love me or maybe I just wasn't good enough. Thirty years later, I discovered that they had wanted to adopt me, but my real mother would not allow it.

This experience explains the deep sense of loss and abandonment that I carried within me for many years. It was imbedded into my subconscious mind along with the belief that wherever I was, I didn't quite belong. I was never really "one of them." This became a pattern that was repeated throughout my life for many years.

By the time I was four-and-a half, I was speaking Ukrainian and called my parents Mama and Tato, mommy and daddy. I felt safe with them, but was always afraid of being left alone. Soon we immigrated to the United States - along with many other families sponsored by a Ukrainian Orthodox church in Detroit, Michigan - where we made our new home. The journey was very traumatic for me, with crowds of people on a big army ship. It was reminiscent of when I was first brought to the DP camps. At every step along the way, I feared being left behind or taken away by someone else. I clung to my parents for dear life.

Adjusting to a new life in America, in a completely new environment with another language, kept me fearful and insecure. Again, I didn't understand the people around me. This solidified in me the belief that at any given moment my life could be turned upside down.

My parents were the only constant in my life, but my refuge and my strength came from retreating into my inner world of being an observer. There I didn't really feel alone. In my own quiet space, I felt protected by some invisible, gentle and loving force that is still with me today. It was an underlying flow of some kind that kept the world moving around me and gave it meaning. It was rather mysterious, maybe even mystical, never frightening, but comforting and very real to me.

I knew my mother wouldn't understand if I tried to ask her about it. Besides, I didn't have the words to explain it. It didn't seem to have anything to do with the rules of right or wrong my parents taught me, rules I always tried to obey. I honored our religious beliefs, attended church every Sunday and believed in God as our Creator and loved and prayed to Jesus Christ. But nothing I was ever taught addressed this "knowing" that I carried within me. I knew that something more existed that kept this world going. I knew it was a good thing and that it had something to do with God.

Since I didn't know how to talk about it, it became my personal "secret friend," my companion, that I talked to all the time. It gave me the strength of internal optimism that carried me through many life challenges. It was there with me when I lost both of my parents at eighteen years old, with a twelve-year-old brother to raise by myself. It has sustained me throughout my life. People have said to me, "You're such a Pollyanna," or "You only see things through rose-colored glasses." But others tell me, "I love your positive uplifting energy. You've given me new hope." This is what I strive to be, a source of inspiration to others.

I eventually came to realize that this source was not only around me, but it has been within me all along. It was a part of me and I was a part of it. It was never anything outside of me, after all. For it is truly the universal God source. It's a forever flowing, pervasive energy of Creation, like the air that we breathe that is part of us all. It is how we are all connected and it is here to help us co-create our lives.

I believe that my connection to this source saved me from the anger and bitterness that my early childhood experiences could have created. Instead it was my greatest teacher. It instilled in me a deep sense of empathy and compassion for the young child's mind and ignited a passion that has never changed. By the time I was seven years old, I knew that I was meant to be a teacher, a guide, a protectress and a "way shower" for the young. I always envisioned myself this way.

My favorite game as a child was school with me as the teacher, of course.

As I matured and my awareness expanded, I realized that we are always children at heart. We carry that child within us, along with all our hopes, joys, sorrows, fears, insecurities, desires, and unfulfilled dreams.

In my own quest to understand my internal world of confusion, disappointments and emotional entrapment, I built a career in education that facilitated my ability to search for the answers and seek out solutions to those things that disturbed and confused me the most.

I discovered that all along, I had not allowed myself to embrace happiness and well-being. Instead, I embraced a belief in struggle, insecurity, fear, poverty, not being good enough, and in not belonging. I demonstrated this by ignoring opportunities and making self-defeating decisions.

This awareness of well-being, along with my determination to make a change, put me on a path to overcome the perceived obstacles that kept me from living the life I desired. As I learned to believe in myself and embrace my own worthiness, doors opened to a whole new truth. The truth is that a world of possibilities lies before me and my mission has just begun.

Professional Experience

Valentina's professional life has focused on human services. This is enhanced by her empathy and enthusiasm for building within others the capacity for positive change.

She started her career life as the founder and administrator of three private Montessori schools, where she created programs for building self-esteem in young children.

Later, Valentina created the first High School Career Resource Center in the state of Michigan, which became a statewide model for other school districts.

As founder of The Job College of Michigan, she contracted with several city governments where she trained and placed hundreds of pink-slipped teachers, laid off government employees, retired executives, and women in transition during a time of extremely high unemployment.

During her nine years as Director of Career Education and Placement at Davenport University in Michigan, Valentina prepared graduate students for a successful career life. She instilled in them, self-confidence and a belief in their own potential, while placing them in the first professional career position.

When Valentina moved to Florida to be close to her family, she enjoyed working for the admissions department at Hodges University where she, again, had the opportunity to inspire college students.

Today, Valentina is founder and director of Swing Star Seminars where she designs and leads professional self-development programs and seminars to inspire people in making positive changes in their lives. She works with professional organizations, small businesses, educators, women's groups, and social service outreach programs.

Her vibrant, yet heart to heart style, inspires others to move into positive action and take charge of their lives. Through her own personal growth and life experience, Valentina is committed to Giving Back by sharing with others her personal insights.

For those interested in taking this manifestation process further, contact Valentina Dimitri at: **valentina@swingstarseminars.com.**

Made in the USA
Monee, IL
28 June 2020

34979995R00138